Guides to Wines &

Beaujolais, Jura, & Savoie

2024 edition

Benjamin Lewin MW

Copyright © 2022, 2023 Benjamin Lewin

ISBN: 9798866514465

Vendange Press

www.vendangepress.com

Without limiting the rights under copyright reserved above, no part of this publication may be reproduced, stored in or introduced into a retrieval system, or transmitted, in any form or by any means (electronic, mechanical, photocopying, recording or otherwise) without the prior written permission of both the copyright owner and the above publisher of the book. All enquiries should be directed to:
contact@vendangepress.com.

Preface

This guide focuses on Beaujolais and Jura-Savoie. The first part of the guide discusses the regions and explains the character and range of the wines, including the characteristics of the individual Crus in Beaujolais and the various regions within the Jura and Savoie. The second part profiles the producers. There are detailed profiles of the leading producers, showing how each winemaker interprets the local character, and mini-profiles of other important estates.

In the first part, I address the nature of the wines made today and ask how this has changed, how it's driven by tradition or competition, and how styles may evolve in the future. I show how the wines are related to the terroir and to the types of grape varieties that are grown, and I explain the classification system. For each region, I suggest reference wines that illustrate the character and variety of the area.

In the second part, there's no single definition for what constitutes a top producer. Leading producers range from those who are so prominent as to represent the common public face of an appellation to those who demonstrate an unexpected potential on a tiny scale. The producers profiled in the guide represent the best of both tradition and innovation in wine in the region. In each profile, I have tried to give a sense of the producer's aims for his wines, of the personality and philosophy behind them—to meet the person who makes the wine, as it were, as much as to review the wines themselves.

Each profile gives contact information and details of production, followed by a description of the producer and the range of wines. For major producers (rated from 1 to 3 stars), I suggest reference wines that are a good starting point for understanding the style. Most of the producers welcome visits, although some require appointments: details are in the profiles. Profiles are organized geographically, and each group of profiles is preceded by maps showing the locations of producers to help plan itineraries.

The guide is based on many visits to the region over recent years. I owe an enormous debt to the many producers who cooperated in this venture by engaging in discussion and opening innumerable bottles for tasting. This guide would not have been possible without them.

Benjamin Lewin

Contents

Overview of Beaujolais	*1*
Production in Beaujolais	*4*
Beaujolais Nouveau	*5*
Beaujolais Crus	*9*
What is the Real Beaujolais?	*17*
Jura	*20*
Savoie	*28*
Vintages	*32*
Visiting the Region	*34*
Profiles of Leading Estates	*37*
Beaujolais	*42*
Jura	*99*
Savoie	*122*
Glossary of French Wine Terms	*135*
Index of Estates by Rating	*138*
Index of Organic and Biodynamic Estates	*139*
Index of Estates by Appellation	*141*
Index of Estates by Name	*143*

Tables

The Beaujolais Crus	*14*
Top Lieu Dits in Beaujolais Crus	*16*
Beaujolais Producers	*20*
Reference Wines for Beaujolais	*19*
Grape Varieties of the Jura	*26*
Reference Wines for the Jura	*28*
Grape Varieties of Savoie	*30*
Crus and Grape Varieties in Savoie	*31*
Reference Wines for Savoie	*32*

Appellation Maps

Beaujolais	*2*
Jura	*22*
Savoie	*29*

Producer Maps

Symbols for Producers	*37*
Beaujolais	*38*
Moulin-à-Vent - Fleurie	*39*
Morgon - Regnié-Durette	*41*
Brouilly	*41*
Jura	*96*
Arbois-Pupillin	*97*
Arlay – Château-Chalon	*98*
Savoie	*120*

Overview of Beaujolais

Beaujolais is a region devoted almost exclusively to a single variety, and for that matter, is close to holding a world monopoly on it. Gamay was common all over Burgundy until the twentieth century, but today has almost disappeared from the region, except for Beaujolais, where it is the sole black grape, and accounts for about 95% of plantings. The other 5% is Chardonnay. Beaujolais accounts for about three quarters of the Gamay in France: the rest is found in the Loire or the Rhône, where it is mostly used to make rosé.

Beaujolais is pretty much the only game in town in the region, as there are few alternative possibilities for red wine. There was a fierce dispute between Beaujolais and Burgundy when it appeared that a loophole in the regulations allowed the labels Bourgogne Rouge and Bourgogne Blanc to be used for wine from Beaujolais. "The Burgundy liner is heading straight for the iceberg of Beaujolais, risking drowning those who paid for the voyage," said a statement issued by the Syndicat des Bourgogne.

Responding to this pressure, the rules were changed in 2011 so that only wine from the Beaujolais Crus can be labeled as Bourgogne, but it must say Bourgogne Gamay if it has more than 30% Gamay (which it always does). The appellation Coteaux Bourguignon, which can be made from Chardonnay or Pinot Noir or Gamay from anywhere in the region, can be used by any red Beaujolais. When the issue was revisited in 2019, with a proposal to allow Pinot Noir from terroirs of limestone in the Beaujolais region to be labeled as Bourgogne, there was a cry of protest: "La Bourgogne c'est la Bourgogne. Et le Beaujolais, c'est le Beaujolais," and the proposal was withdrawn.

Beaujolais falls into three areas. The entire region is entitled to use the description, Beaujolais, but most of the wine labeled as Beaujolais AOP comes from the southern part. The higher level of Beaujolais Villages comes from the northern part. Unlike the Côtes du Rhône, where the Villages AOP consists of islands surrounded by the generic appellation, Beaujolais Villages is a large, contiguous area. Within it are the ten "crus," each of which is entitled to label its wine solely with the name of the cru.

"Classification in Beaujolais is a matter of granite," said Georges Duboeuf. This is the distinction between the areas of Beaujolais and

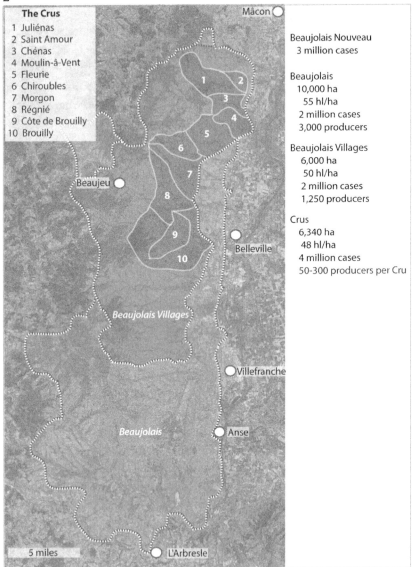

Beaujolais AOP largely occupies the southern part of the area. Beaujolais Villages is the northern part, and the crus are located within the Villages region.

Beaujolais Villages. A band of granite runs between Mâcon and Villefranche, and more or less fills the width of the Beaujolais Villages. The terrain in the Beaujolais AOP to the south is a mix of sedimentary clay and some limestone.

A view of the hills of the Beaujolais from Croix de Rochefort. Courtesy Beaujolais Vignoble.

There is general agreement that Gamay does best on granite. As Gamay is not very widely grown, there isn't much experience in comparing its results on a variety of terroirs. But I suspect that it's not so much that granite is especially suitable for Gamay (rather than other grape varieties), but that it brings a tautness needed to counteract a natural tendency to show blowsy fruits.

Gamay should not be heavy: until the past decade or so, chaptalization was something of a problem in giving the wines an artificial weight. "A lot of people in Beaujolais feel that if you don't have 13% alcohol, your wine won't age; people make a connection between alcohol and quality, but I think that's a big mistake," says Louis-Benoît Desvignes in Morgon. Warmer vintages, and an especially good run from 2009 to 2015, mean that lately much more of the alcohol has been natural.

Driving through the vineyards, Beaujolais looks different from other regions, because most vineyards follow the old tradition of pruning vines as free-standing bushes. There's a slow move to a more modern trellis system. "The gobelet (local name for the bush) made it easy to protect the vine in winter by heaping earth around, and in cooler summers the soil reflected light up. But honestly, with the winters and summers we have now, we think it's better to have a trellis," said former winemaker Cyril Chirouze at Jadot's Château des Jacques. He believes changes will be necessary to respond to global warming. "The most important thing is to change the system of growing, to have more leaves, to be able to adapt to hot conditions. I am more convinced about the need for a change in viticulture than a change in grape varieties. We have to make a lot of changes in the vineyards to make Gamay able to withstand the warmer conditions."

The small amount of white wine that is made in Beaujolais comes from Chardonnay. Some of the villages in Beaujolais can label white wine as Bourgogne Blanc, but otherwise it must be labeled as Beaujolais Blanc. "I think it's very important that Chardonnay continues to be planted in Beaujolais because it is part of our complexity," says Cyril Chirouze. "Beaujolais should not be considered as a homogeneous region. It has a lot of different terroirs, and rosé and white wine as well as red." Château des Jacques produces both Bourgogne Blanc and Beaujolais Blanc, and Cyril draws an interesting distinction between them. "The Bourgogne Blanc has winemaking that's close to Burgundy; half is fermented in barriques. The Beaujolais Blanc is made exclusively in stainless steel."

Production in Beaujolais

Beaujolais has been in crisis for the past half century. Production of Beaujolais has more than halved since 1999, Beaujolais Villages has fallen almost as much, and the crus have fared only a little better. Part of the problem is a perception that Beaujolais means low quality. Indeed, a local magazine, *Lyon Mag*, published an interview with oenologist François Mauss in 2002 under the title "Le Beaujolais, c'est de la merde." The producers did the worst possible thing: they sued for libel. They won a decidedly pyrrhic victory; the resulting publicity did nothing to help Beaujolais. (The award was subsequently overturned on appeal.)

Most Beaujolais vineyards are pruned with the free-standing gobelet bush.

Beaujolais production really falls into four categories: independent producers; cooperatives; negociants; and Georges Duboeuf. Although they are the driving force for innovation, independent producers are the smallest part of the mix. Cooperatives account for more than a third of production. The negociant scene has been changing as the large negociants in Burgundy, just to the north, have seen value in Beaujolais, and have been acquiring the local houses (and sometimes also land). All this may lead to an improvement in quality.

For many the region is synonymous with Georges Duboeuf, known for his remarkable palate and eye for quality, who established a negociant business in the Beaujolais in 1964. "My ancestors were vignerons at Chaintré for four centuries. I inherited 4 ha of vineyards at Pouilly-Fuissé, not very large, but I was sure of the quality of my wine and started by selling Pouilly-Fuissé everywhere. People said to me, the Pouilly-Fuissé is very good, but we need a good red. So I started to buy and bottle wine," is how Georges recollected the beginning. "Hameau Duboeuf," as his winery at Romanèche-Thorins is now signposted, has become a vast enterprise.

By far the largest producer of Beaujolais Nouveau, Duboeuf alone is responsible for a significant part of all Beaujolais production, buying grapes (but no longer wine) from more than 400 growers. Reports variously place Duboeuf's share of all Beaujolais production between 20% and 40%—"Yes, it's something like that," says export manager Romain Teyteau offhandedly when asked for the exact figure. Total production is probably actually around 15-20% of Beaujolais' total of 100 million bottles. While Duboeuf is ineradicably associated with Beaujolais Nouveau, he also produces Beaujolais, Beaujolais Villages, and an extensive series of wines from all the crus, including a substantial number of single vineyard cuvées.

Beaujolais Nouveau

"The most difficult to vinify of all the wines is Beaujolais Nouveau, because it is very fast and depends on technique," Georges said. Beaujolais Nouveau has been at once the resurrection and the downfall of Beaujolais. Beaujolais has always been sold young: called Beaujolais Primeur, through the nineteenth century it was often sold as barrels in which the wine was still fermenting. By the time it reached its destina-

6

tion, it was ready to sell to the consumer! In the twentieth century it was released early in the bistros of nearby Lyon. The rule today is that Nouveau wine can be shipped from the second Thursday in November in order to be available worldwide for sale a week later. (This is a month earlier than for Beaujolais AOP.)

Beaujolais Nouveau was about 10% of all production when it first became known by this name in the 1950s. Production of Beaujolais doubled by the 1980s, and Nouveau increased to more than a quarter. At the peak it was significantly more than half of all production, but today it's in decline. Sales are falling worldwide, except for Japan, where the rhythm of the annual ritual remains appealing.

In its time, Beaujolais Nouveau was a lifesaver. Sales of Beaujolais were depressed through the 1950s, and the novelty, or perhaps one might say the gimmick, of Beaujolais Nouveau gave a much-needed lift. Beaujolais Nouveau has always been a marketing phenomenon. Races to get the first Beaujolais Nouveau to Paris or to London by unusual means attracted publicity, at its peak involving a hoopla of balloons, parachutes, racing cars, or even supersonic Concord at the end of the century. The slogan "Le Beaujolais Nouveau est Arrivé" became so effective that it was a rare wine shop that did not have it on a placard in the window on November 15.

Nouveau solved a problem by making something that was acceptable to consumers from vineyards that had not been able to succeed with more conventional wine. But the solution lasted only so long as Beaujolais Nouveau was in vogue. The more general problem is not really with Beaujolais Nouveau as such, but with collateral damage. Beaujolais Nouveau is certainly different from other wine; fermentation has barely finished when the wine is bottled, and it might more appropriately be called "fermented grape juice" than wine. But it dominates the image of Beaujolais. Fresh, tart, and (sometimes) fruity, with the aromas of fermentation still much in evidence, it needs to be drunk within a few weeks. Most Beaujolais has always been made for early drinking, but Beaujolais Nouveau is the extreme case.

During the 1970s and 1980s, when the phenomenon peaked, Beaujolais Nouveau really pulled the region out of trouble. But its reputation among more serious wine drinkers is terrible. "The Nouveau has destroyed our image. All of Beaujolais is confused with Nouveau," says

The dispatch of the new vintage of Beaujolais was a sedate affair early in the twentieth century (around 1917).

Jean-Pierre Large, director of Domaine Cheysson in Chiroubles, pointing to the problem that putting "Beaujolais" on the label is tantamount to telling the consumer that quality (and price) must be limited. "The reputation of Beaujolais is very bad because of Beaujolais Nouveau. But Beaujolais and Beaujolais Villages are made in the same way as the crus," says Baptiste Condemine at Domaine des Souchons. The basic problem is that anything with Beaujolais on the label is stamped with the impression created by Beaujolais Nouveau.

With the exception of some top wines from the crus, Beaujolais is made by a method called semi-carbonic maceration. This requires the vats to be filled with whole clusters of berries (so there is no destemming). Fermentation takes place within the berries, releasing carbon dioxide, which maintains an oxygen-free atmosphere. This is carbonic maceration. However, juice is released from berries that are broken, and the stems form a network allowing the juice to surround the berries. The juice also ferments (conventionally, catalyzed by yeast), so the overall process is called semi-carbonic maceration.

Typically when the process is about half complete, the free juice is run off, the remaining berries are pressed, the free-run and pressed juice are combined, and fermentation is completed just like for any red wine. The minimal exposure of the juice to the skins means that little tannin is extracted, so that simple fruit flavors dominate the wine, which tends to have a bright purple color. The extent of carbonic maceration is deter-

One of the more successful stunts for presenting Beaujolais Nouveau was a motorcycle cavalcade of chefs through New York led by Franck Duboeuf in November 2008. Courtesy Melanie Young.

mined by the proportion of whole clusters and the length of time before pressing; it is greatest for Nouveau and least for the crus.

The key feature of Beaujolais Nouveau is its immediate fruitiness. Somewhat controversially, the style has been enhanced by the use of thermovinification. As used in Beaujolais, this involves heating berries to 55°C for 8-12 hours and then cooling them down for fermentation. "This is very current here. It increases color and aromatics. It's mostly used for nouveau and a little bit for Beaujolais and Villages. It's especially useful when the quality of the grapes is not so good," explains oenologist Denis Lapalu at Duboeuf. "It's indispensable in a year such as 2012, it's very much a function of the vintage. Without it we would not be able to achieve the quality in some years," Georges Duboeuf added.

Thermovinification is controversial because it strengthens the impression of fermentation aromatics. "Unfortunately 90% of Beaujolais today is made by thermovinification—it's terrible," says Mathieu Lapierre of Domaine Marcel Lapierre in Morgon. The question is really what you want from Beaujolais Nouveau. It's never going to represent terroir.

"In Beaujolais we go from catastrophe to catastrophe. Twenty years ago there were yeasts that made the wine aromatic, hiding the terroir. Today thermovinification is a catastrophe; it's a technique for giving aromas of cassis—but it does it equally for wines from limestone or granite, from Brouilly or Moulin-à-Vent. It does not correspond at all to the idea that the vigneron makes wine to express his vines. It's industrial

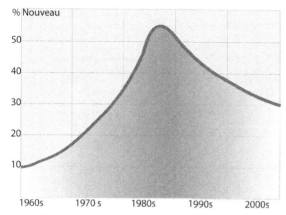

Beaujolais Nouveau rose from a level of 10% in 1960 to a peak of 55% in 1986 before falling to its present 30% of all Beaujolais.

wine made by technological methods," says Jean-Paul Brun at Domaine des Terres Dorées. Growers who focus on crus agree. "The difference between crus has disappeared at the negociants and producers who are using thermovinification. It started in Beaujolais for handling grapes that had problems, for example, damaged by hail, and allowed you to make decent wine; but at the same time it destroyed the best wine. I don't understand how it's possible to do this within the appellation rules, because it destroys the differences between appellations," says Louis-Benoît Desvignes.

Up to half of production from the Beaujolais AOP is Nouveau. Up to a third of Beaujolais Villages is produced as Nouveau, but the crus are not allowed to produce Nouveau. Nouveau is intended for immediate consumption, Beaujolais and Beaujolais Villages should be drunk within a year or so, but some of the crus make wines with ageworthiness.

Beaujolais Crus

"You have to dissociate the crus from Beaujolais. They are apart. There are people who drink only the crus and there are people who drink only Beaujolais Nouveau. The crus are distinguished by terroir and vintage, which is different from Nouveau. One speaks of 2009 as a great vintage, 2010 is different, and so on. Moulin-à-Vent has a reputation more like Burgundy," Georges Duboeuf explained.

The crus are allowed to put the name of the cru alone on the bottle (without mentioning Beaujolais), and often do so to minimize the connection with Beaujolais. While this may be helpful for the crus, of course

The most famous cru of Beaujolais, Moulin-à-Vent, takes its name from the old windmill. Extending from Chénas to Romanèche-Thorins, it is the only Cru not be named after a village. It has 640 ha divided into 15 climats, and 280 producers.

it denies the rest of the Beaujolais any uplift from the halo of its best wines.

The crus offer a wide range of qualities, from wine just above Villages standard, to the top wines of Morgon or Moulin-à-Vent, which may be made by conventional vinification and have aging potential. At their best, these can resemble the Côte d'Or. Not everyone approves of this. "I do not think they are necessarily any better for it," said Clive Coates MW. "Good Beaujolais... is a light red wine, not at all tannic, purple in color, abundantly fruity and not a bit heavy or sweet." Yet Beaujolais is moving in the direction of weightier wines. "It's very important for us to show that Beaujolais can age," says Anthon Collet of the producers' association, Inter Beaujolais.

It's a mistake to regard the best crus as ready for drinking upon release. Those from the top producers need at least another year or so. Perhaps in an exceptional year like 2009 the fruits immediately outweigh the structure, but otherwise there can be enough tannin to obscure the fruits. For the best wines in a good year, the ideal period may be to enjoy them around five years after the vintage; it is only an exceptional wine—perhaps a top Moulin-à-Vent or Morgon—that is likely to last longer than that. At their best, the top crus can be difficult to distinguish from village wines from the Côte de Beaune.

Morgon has 1,100 ha and 6 climats. Its best climat, Côte du Py, is a steep hill with a plateau at the top marked by a cross with an inscription that says, "Erected in grateful recognition of the extraordinary harvest of 1906."

But there is a great range even within the top crus. One of the problems in Beaujolais is that the attempts to make wines with complexity and aging potential from the crus is undercut by wines with prices barely above Beaujolais Villages. As in Burgundy, the producer is the only reliable guide.

Maybe it's time for another revolution, and perhaps the recent study of terroirs, represented on the walls of many producers by copies of the multicolored maps showing the soil types in the Crus, has been a contributory factor. Twenty years ago, most producers would have one, or at most two, cuvées from a Cru. Now it's common to find multiple cuvées from each Cru, each representing specific terroir. About a quarter of the wines from the Crus now carry the name of a lieu-dit.

The maps are the result of extensive land surveys to support the argument for premier crus, with several candidates in Moulin-à-Vent, Fleurie, and Morgon. In Fleurie the best known *climat* is La Madone, the hill with the emblematic chapel on top. In Morgon, it is Côte du Py, a hill that rises to 350m. In Moulin-à-Vent, the windmill marks the spot: the four best-known *climats* extend around the hill and just below the windmill. Actually, 160 lieu-dits were mapped and classed into five levels on a map drawn up by Budker in 1901; the assignments are still quite accurate.

Fleurie's symbol is La Madone, a small chapel on top of a hill (300m) that can be seen from all over the appellation. Fleurie has 830 ha and 13 climats. Grille-Midi is the top climat.

Individual cuvées are a recent phenomenon. It's a sign of how things are changing that Louis-Benoît Desvignes recollects, "When I started a special bottling (the Vieilles Vignes from Javernières on the Côte du Py) in 2009, people thought I would lose customers." At Château des Jacques, whose vineyards are just below the famous windmill in Moulin-à-Vent, six individual vineyard cuvées have been added to the general blend (which for years was in any case the best wine of the appellation).

There are mixed feelings about the change that premier crus will bring. "In the next five to ten years we will definitely have premier crus. The locomotive is Morgon and Moulin-à-Vent. But it will be both good and bad. People from Burgundy come here to buy land—it's speculation. I'm a peasant, I'm not a financier. The price of land and the wine will increase," Louis-Benoît says. Yet to some extent, an important transition has already taken place with the increasing move toward single vineyard wines by several producers. Recognition of premier crus may simply formalize the premium that already is being paid for the best sites. The first formal proposal is from Fleurie, which has asked for 7 of its 48 lieudits to be classified as premier crus.

It's ironic that the attempt to define premier crus coincides with the effects of climate change. Export manager Romain Teyteau at Georges Duboeuf says that, "The key to the future is to keep freshness. On Côte de

Rising to 520m, with slopes up to 40%, Mont Brouilly dominates the southern end of the Crus. Brouilly has 1,250 ha and Côte de Brouilly has 320 ha.

Brouilly, the best terroir used to be the south slope, but now it's the north slope."

"Morgon is the oldest cru of Beaujolais. It was the first because it had the history, it's the best. There's lots of schist. There are 6 climats. Studies of soils and subsoils have been done to define the areas; there will be premier crus in a few years," says Baptiste Condemine at Domaine des Souchons. But he adds, "Many people know Morgon because they know Marcel Lapierre. I think this is more important for us than premier crus."

Indeed Marcel Lapierre was at the forefront of a revolution led by the "gang of four" (the name given them by their American importer, Kermit Lynch). The others were Guy Breton, Jean-Paul Thévenet, and Jean Foillard, all friends from the town of Villié-Morgon. Their impetus came from a winemaker called Jules Chauvet, who introduced them to the notion of picking late for full ripeness, selecting to eliminate rotten berries, using natural yeast, minimizing sulfur dioxide, using slow fermentation at low temperature (the proportion of carbonic maceration varies with producer and vintage), and maturing in barriques.

"My father was part of a group that rebelled against the industrial production of Beaujolais," says Mathieu Lapierre, adding, "We try to make natural wines but it's difficult to defend them from the industrial system. We try to master things so as to be as natural as possible, but no one can be superman." It's a measure of his attitude that when asked about global warming, he says, "I'm not sure about that, the real question

The Beaujolais Crus	
Brouilly is one of the weaker Crus, and it can be difficult to find wines that really stand out above Beaujolais Villages.	*1,250 ha* *46% granite* *530 growers*
Côte de Brouilly describes the steep slopes of the ancient volcano of Mont Brouilly, and is a step up above Brouilly. Soils are based on the hard blue-green rock, diorite (40% of area); this is one of the least granitic Crus..	*320 ha* *24% granite* *50 growers*
Chénas is the smallest Cru. The wines are solid without reaching the interest level of the top Crus. Soils are mostly Piedmont deposits (mountain debris).	*260 ha* *47% granite* *100 growers*
Chiroubles has the highest elevation, with the steepest slopes, the coolest climate of the Crus, typically harvesting a week later than the other Crus.	*360 ha* *100% granite* *60 growers*
Fleurie, sometimes called the Queen of Beaujolais, is the most generous and fleshy. The sun-exposed area of Grille-Midi is its top area. Wines from the La Roilette area adjacent to Moulin à Vent can be more structured. The granite is pink.	*830 ha* *90% granite* *180 growers*
Juliénas has the least granite of the Crus; it's rich in volcanic blue rocks called diorite in the west (42% of terroir), and is more sedimentary in the east. Slopes are relatively steep and have the greatest exposure to the south. It is sturdier than most Crus, and can be a little hard.	*570 ha* *3% granite* *120 growers*
Morgon traditionally is regarded as taking second place after Moulin à Vent as the most structured Cru, but recently it may have overtaken it, especially with the climat of the Côte du Py, where the volcanic soils tend to be more mineral than Moulin à Vent. A concentration of good producers makes it one of the most reliable Crus.	*1,100 ha* *52% granite* *250 growers*
Moulin à Vent, often called the King of Beaujolais, is the most powerful and structured Cru. This is sometimes attributed to manganese and iron in the soil. It's the most homogeneous of the Crus.	*640 ha* *53% granite* *280 growers*
Regnié is known for its pink granite. Wines are lighter than the top Crus (it became a Cru only in 1988).	*390 ha* *64% granite* *80 growers*
Saint Amour is the most northern Cru, at the border with Mâcon. Vineyards are less steep, on more varied and less granitic soils. Wines are the lightest of the Crus, with a fresh quality just a tad above Beaujolais Villages.	*330 ha* *22% granite* *115 growers*

is why some people in Beaujolais chaptalize; if you reach 12% do you need more alcohol?"

15

So what is the difference in the crus? A single word describes the difference with the average Beaujolais: structure. This is not to imply that the wines are tough, but behind the fruits is the necessary framework to support development.

"The difference between the crus is the terroir. Brouilly is blue stone, Fleurie is pink granite, and Moulin-à-Vent has manganese. The crus are an element in advancing the reputation of the region," said Georges Duboeuf. A tasting with Georges is an education in Beaujolais. Starting with the Beaujolais Villages, the wine is all about fruit. "This is the side of Beaujolais we all like, very juicy and fruity," he said. "You get fruit and freshness and for another year or two you will be able to enjoy it. What we are looking for in Beaujolais Villages is the pleasure of the moment." The distinction between Beaujolais Villages and the lesser crus is the more direct sense of fruit aromatics in the Villages (often reflecting more carbonic maceration). The Crus cannot be sold until March 15 after the harvest (compared to December 15 for Beaujolais and Beaujolais Villages), but there is an exception for Saint Amour, which because of its name is popular for Valentine's Day.

The lightest Crus, often barely distinguished from better Beaujolais Villages, are Brouilly (the largest), Regnié, and Saint Amour. On the slopes of Mont Brouilly, Côte de Brouilly is distinct from Brouilly; and with even more elevation, Chiroubles comes from hillside vineyards often over 300m. Tasting with Duboeuf, the flavor spectrum of Brouilly and Chiroubles are generally similar, with more weight than the Villages, but less evident aromatics. Chénas is solid. Then going up the scale of crus, there is more intensity, but not a great change in character. The real difference comes when you reach Morgon, Fleurie, and Moulin-à-Vent. Morgon is taut, Fleurie is soft and fleshy, and Moulin-à-Vent is quite serious and elegant.

Morgon and Moulin-à-Vent have the most distinctive soils, with manganese prominent in both, and iron in the latter. They often seem more Burgundian as they age. Fleurie can be immediately appealing; although vineyards close to Morgon or Moulin-à-Vent sometimes take on the more structured quality of those appellations, in the heart of the appellation, the wines are fleshy. The old description was that Fleurie is the queen of Beaujolais, while Moulin-à-Vent is the king. Morgon has varied terroirs, from the sandier soil of Corcelette, to the more alluvial soil and greater clay of Grand Cras, to volcanic terroir on Côte du Py.

Best-Known Lieu Dits in Beaujolais Crus

Cru	Lieu Dit	Terroir
Chiroubles	Javernand	high elevation with some sand in the soil
	La Madone	the top of the hill with shallow soils of granite; the emblematic lieu-dit
Fleurie	Grille-Midi	warm amphitheater in the south facing the sun
	Les Moriers	northeast quadrant with granite and quartz
Juliénas	Les Capitans	schist and basalt in the center of the cru
Morgon	Côte de Py	at the top of an extinct volcano, facing southeast
	Javernières	continuation of Côte de Py to the east, with deep blue granite
	Les Thorins	the hill where the windmill stands; historically the top lieu-dit
Moulin-à-Vent	La Roche	immediately below the windmill
	Le Carquelin	sandy soil with high concentration of manganese on top of granite
	Rochegrès	between Les Thorins and Chènas, granite with manganese

Moulin-à-Vent always has structure, but if you really want to taste the character that granite gives wine, go to Morgon, especially the Côte du Py, which shows that taut restraint of granite. It is the most distinctive of the crus. Juliénas, which can be a big, sturdy wine, comes as a surprise, placed in Duboeuf's lineup after the Moulin-à-Vent: while tight and structured, it doesn't have the same tensile impression as Morgon or Moulin-à-Vent. The differences as you ascend the hierarchy are more to do with the balance between fruits and acidity, breadth versus tautness, or intensity of concentration, than the flavor spectrum as such.

Fleurie and Moulin-à-Vent have always been considered ahead of all the other crus, but I would now place Morgon with them. One reason is that young winemakers, who bring new, modern attitudes to the region, such as Julien Sunier or Mee Godard, can more easily buy land in Morgon, where prices are only about two thirds of Fleurie or Moulin-à-Vent. Perhaps this is associated with the increased emphasis on climats in Morgon, which is bringing its terroirs into sharper focus.

Lapierre's Morgon can in fact be a little hard in the first year or so, but four years after a great vintage, it shows tense black fruits with earthy overtones, and a real sense of terroir that might be confused, for example, with Pommard. "Morgon should have an aroma of violets and cherries, with flavors of strawberries and a slightly masculine side," says Mathieu. Morgon is serious wine, often giving a taut impression of its granitic terroir, with the greatest purity of line usually to be found in the putative premier cru of Côte du Py.

What is the Real Beaujolais?

The tradition in the region is to mature the wine—even the crus—in cement tanks. Slowly wood has been introduced. Château des Jacques in Moulin-à-Vent—always one of the most ageworthy wines—has done this for decades, and the trend has been accentuated since Jadot acquired the estate in 1996. While initially regarded with some scepticism by others, today there is a definite move in this direction, and many producers in the top crus now have at least one cuvée that is matured in barriques.

Vinification should be a bigger issue than it is: carbonic maceration is regarded as traditional, but actually it's a twentieth century phenomenon. "Carbonic maceration started to be used only in the 1950s. Until then, wine making in Beaujolais was very similar to Burgundy," said Cyril Chirouze at Château des Jacques. "So we consider that the real tradition is to work like Burgundy."

Carbonic maceration is the lifeblood for Beaujolais Nouveau, and is probably necessary for Beaujolais and Beaujolais Villages: would Burgundian precepts make better wines for the Crus? The risk with carbonic maceration is that the wine seems superficial, driven by high-toned aromatics in the absence of tannins. This can be lovely for immediate enjoyment, but carbonic maceration is not a technique that brings out terroir differences, so it's somewhat at odds with a move towards defining a hierarchy of premier crus within the top crus. Export manager Romain Teyteau at Georges Duboeuf concedes that, "Some people feel that carbonic maceration undermines terroir, but it's what gives Beaujolais its special character." He adds, "We like Beaujolais that tastes like Beaujolais, not to mimic other regions."

So what is the real Beaujolais, where is the future of the region? In wines using carbonic maceration to bring out fruits or in wines made

Beaujolais Producers

Traditional producers
Semi-carbonic maceration and aging in cuve

David-Beaupère	Bernard Diochon
Domaine des Billards	Domaine de la Grand'Cour
Jean-Marc Burgaud	Paul Janin et Fils
Joseph Chamonard	Yvon Métras
Domaine de la Chaponne	Métrat et Fils
Chignard	Domaine des Nugues
Damien Coquelet	Coudert Clos de La Roilette
Georges Descombes	Domaine des Souchons
Louis et Claude Desvignes	Château Thivin

"Mixed" producers
Some semi-carbonic maceration, some aging in barriques

Guy Breton	Marcel Lapierre
Clos du Fief	Julien Sunier
Jules Desjourneys	Charly Thévenet
Jean-Claude Lapalu	Jean-Paul Thévenet

"Burgundian" producers
Destemming, conventional fermentation, and aging in barriques

Daniel Bouland	Lafarge-Vial
Château Grange Cochard	Terres Dorées
Mee Godard	Thibault Liger-Belair
Château des Jacques	Domaine Thillardon

The Large Negociants

Georges Duboeuf	Dominique Piron
Henry Fessy	Maison Trénel

Descriptions of style are only approximate, because some producers use more than one style, typically traditional for Beaujolais or lesser Crus, moving towards Burgundian for the top Crus.

more conventionally to balance fruits with structure? Jean-Paul Brun at Domaine des Terres Dorées has had difficulties with his attempts to obtain the AOP agrément for ageworthy wines. He does not use carbonic maceration for any of his wines, not even the Beaujolais. "If you use carbonic maceration it's too short to allow the terroir to express itself. Burgundian vinification for all the wines lasts for 5-6 weeks. A Burgundian vinification has the objective of transmitting the terroir to the wine." If Beaujolais is truly to find a way forward through the classification of

Reference Wines for Beaujolais	
Beaujolais	Domaine des Terres Dorées, L'Ancien
Beaujolais Villages	Georges Duboeuf
Brouilly	Jean-Claude Lapalu, Vieilles Vignes Georges Descombes
Chénas	Paul-Henri Thillardon
Chiroubles	Patrick Bouland
Côte de Brouilly	Domaine des Terres Dorées Château Thivin
Fleurie	Yvon Métras
Juliénas	Georges Duboeuf, Château des Capitans Clos du Fief
Morgon	Marcel Lapierre
Morgon, Côte du Py	Louis & Claude Desvignes Jean Foillard
Moulin-à-Vent	Château des Jacques
Regnié	Charly Thévenet
St. Amour	Maison Trénel

premier crus, it's beyond time to stop making difficulties for producers who are making the very wines that should prove the point.

Of course, few people ask the most fundamental question, which is all but unthinkable: is Gamay the best grape to grow in the Beaujolais? Is it time to recognize that it's a historical accident that Gamay became the grape of Beaujolais, more faute de mieux than anything else; should we step back and ask what grape variety would actually make the best wine here?

The grape that thrives on granite par excellence is Syrah; and the warming climate has brought Beaujolais close to the temperatures of the Northern Rhône, say, three decades ago. It would not be surprising if Syrah did well in the areas of the top Crus. Some producers have been planting trial plots of Syrah. Château des Jacques planted a hectare of Syrah in 2015, for producing a Vin de France. "The idea is not that we will use a lot of Syrah, it is just to be curious," says Cyril Chirouze. A little

20

more forcefully, as is his style, Jean-Charles Boisset from Burgundy has planted Syrah in a vineyard owned by one of his negociants, Mommessin; the wine is sold as a Vin de France.

Others feel that Burgundy should be the model: "Syrah is a beautiful variety, but Gamay is much better, it's more approachable," says Louis-Clément David-Beaupère. "We are a much more Burgundian producer than the Rhone valley, and Gamay is our identity." In another twist on this view, Burgundian negociant Louis Latour has planted a 44 ha vineyard of Pinot Noir at the southern end of Beaujolais. The wine is labeled as Coteaux Bourguignon.

The future is unclear. The practical difficulty is whether there is any alternative for the vineyards that are now producing Beaujolais Nouveau. Needless to say, these are not the best vineyards. Perhaps it's better that they produce Beaujolais Nouveau rather than join the lake of wine to be distilled, but the price is to devalue the reputation of the rest of Beaujolais. "Beaujolais Nouveau is one of the most incredible ideas of the twentieth century. People of my generation don't know that we have crus in Beaujolais—it's crazy," says Louis-Benoît Desvignes. Admittedly, the crus vary from wines that are barely distinguishable from Beaujolais Villages to those that might be confused with reds from the Côte de Beaune, but the best are some of the few remaining undiscovered bargains from the region.

Jura

Jura-Savoie are usually lumped together as those regions which do not fit into Burgundy or the Rhône, but the regions are well separated and the connection is slight. The terroirs are different: Jura has rolling hills and Savoie has the grandeur of the mountains. The grape varieties are different. And there is little commonality of style. Savoie is dominated by indigenous varieties, mostly white. The Jura is caught between vinification of the Savagnin grape in an oxidative style producing wine akin to Sherry, contrasted with wines made in the modern style from Savagnin or Chardonnay.

The Jura has generally been fairly obscure, with wine made by local producers on a relatively small scale, and not much interest from negociants from elsewhere, but recently there's been a small move into the region by producers from Burgundy.

About fifty miles east of Burgundy, the Jura is separated from the Côte d'Or by the valley of the Saône river. Vineyards in the Jura are more elevated (around 250-400m), on slopes that face west or south-west. Soils are clay and limestone, with outbreaks of marl (limestone-rich mud). There is more clay in the Jura than in Burgundy, because when the massif of the Jura advanced towards Burgundy, clay was pushed up to the surface at the base of the foothills, whereas in Burgundy it remains underground. Cooler than Burgundy, and with more rain, the climate is marginal for wine growing.

Côtes de Jura is the general AOP for the region; within it the Arbois AOP is far larger than the small AOPs of Château-Chalon (this is the name of the AOP not a producer) and l'Etoile. There is also a tiny appellation of Arbois-Pupillin, just 300 ha on steep slopes above the village of Pupillin. In addition, there are two AOPs for specific wine styles: Crémant de Jura and Macvin (a sweet vin de liqueur made by adding spirits to stop fermentation early).

In steady decline ever since phylloxera, when there were around 20,000 ha of vineyards, plantings in the Jura have now stabilized at under 2,000 ha, with almost all vineyards in one of the AOPs. Only five grape varieties are allowed in the AOPs: Chardonnay and Savagnin for the whites; and Poulsard, Trousseau, and Pinot Noir for the blacks. The trend is towards increasing production of white wines, which today are about two thirds of production (including sparkling as well as still wines).

Reflecting the symmetry with Burgundy across the Saône valley, Chardonnay is the predominant variety, accounting for about half of all plantings. It is not a newcomer here, having been grown for several cen-

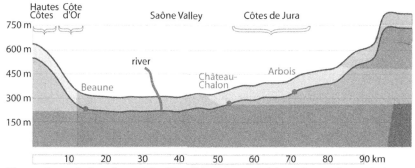

The southeast-facing slope of the Côte d'Or is separated from the southwest-facing slopes of the Jura by the valley of the Saône.

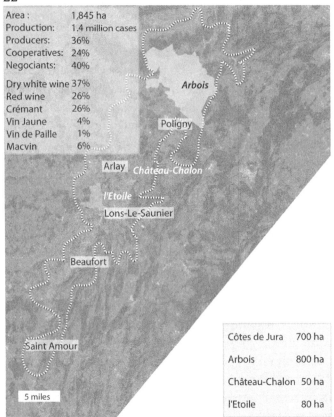

The individual appellations of Arbois, Château-Chalon, and l'Etoile are relatively compact, but the Côtes de Jura extends over 50 miles.

turies under a variety of local names. "People say, oh, now you are making Chardonnay in the Jura, but Chardonnay has been grown here for a very long time—some speak of the fourteenth century," says Stéphane Tissot. Yet in terms of stylistic imperatives, it is Savagnin that makes the running.

The local myth is that Savagnin was imported from Tokaji in Hungary in the Middle Ages. In fact, its origins are in the other direction, as it is the same variety as Gewürztraminer in Alsace, yet in the Jura it gives a wine with pronounced savory quality, rather than the floral perfume of Gewürztraminer. Essentially Savagnin is a nonaromatic variant and Gewürztraminer is an aromatic variant of the variety. Savagnin or Chardonnay show a similar savory thread, as do wines blended from the two varieties.

The traditional style in the Jura allows wine to mature in barriques that are not topped up. Yeast grow on the surface of the wine to form a voile (as seen here in a white layer about an inch deep).

It seems that the Jura has suddenly been discovered for the unusual character of its wines. "Five years ago it was easy to buy vines here, now it's difficult, the wines are having a great success and people don't want to sell," says Jacques Duvivier, who has come to Arbois to run the Marquis d'Angerville's expansion from Volnay into the Jura. "In the Jura we have specific soils and specific varieties, and we have to show that. The Jura is successful because it is original."

The Jura's claim to fame comes from its oxidative style, almost unique in France. (Similar techniques are used in Gaillac for its *vin de voile*). Traditional winemaking used old barriques, but did not fill them completely or top up to compensate for loss by evaporation. The result is that a layer of yeast, known locally as the *voile* (veil), grows on the surface of the wine. Producers are quick to tell you that the yeasts aren't the same as those forming the *flor* on fino Sherry, but the principle is the same, and the results are similar. (Sherry is fortified but the Jura wines are natural, although evaporation during maturation can increase alcohol to a similar level.)

The layer of yeast is thinner in the Jura, and more gray in hue. It protects the maturing wine from becoming oxidized to vinegar, and contributes a distinctive aroma and flavor. The wine has a taut, savory quality with distinct dryness on the finish (because the yeasts consume glycerol). The main aromatic characteristics are the production of acetaldehyde (an oxidized product of ethanol), which gives a faintly nutty character, and sotolon, an aromatic, spicy compound that contributes

24

curry-like notes. In fact, sotolon is also a product of the fenugreek plant, whose seeds are used in Madras curry.

The antithesis of the modern trend to fruit-driven wines, the oxidative style is an acquired taste that has been going out of fashion. As a result, most producers now also make wines in a modern, which is to say non-oxidative, style. The most common term used to describe these wines is ouillé (from ouillage, meaning topping-up). Wines in the oxidative style are most often described as traditional or vinifié sous voile (or sometimes typé). The distinction is a recent development: "The production of wines in the ouillé style at Château-Chalon started only around 1990," says Jean Berthet-Bondet, one of the leading producers.

Some old-line producers have eschewed the ouillé style, but it's a sign of the times that Laurent Macle, from one of the most traditional producers in Château-Chalon, produced his first ouillé wine in 2007. It's only four barrels, but a source of argument as Laurent's father does not approve. "He will never be convinced," says Laurent, who believes this may be the true expression of terroir. "People confuse terroir with the taste of Vin Jaune (vinifié sous voile), but it's the aging that gives the wine its flavor."

The most fascinating aspect of the Jura is a sense of convergence between the oxidized and ouillé styles, and between Chardonnay and Savagnin. Even in the ouillé style, Chardonnay sometimes takes on a more savory quality, faintly reminiscent of Savagnin in its oxidized style. Walking in the vineyards, I was convinced I could smell fenugreek on the air. But it's more likely that the presence of both types of wine in the same cellar is responsible.

A tasting with Stéphane Tissot at Domaine André & Mireille Tissot provided an interesting comparison. The Traminer and Savagnin cuvées come from the same vines, but the names of the cuvées indicate different types of vinification. Traminer is nonoxidative, but Savagnin has 30 months under voile. Even the first shows some savory influences, but they are much stronger in the second. One seems more like an extreme example of the other, rather than completely different.

Wines in the oxidative style go back at least to the eighteenth century, and the epitome of the style is Vin Jaune, which matures in barrique under a voile for six years. Vin Jaune comes exclusively from Savagnin. For most appellations it is one of several wine styles that can be produced, but Château-Chalon produces only Vin Jaune, and is usually considered

Château-Chalon is located at a high point on a plateau overlooking the vineyards of the appellation down below. Soils of blue marl retain heat, and the vineyards are protected from the wind by south-southwest exposure.

to provide its peak expression. (Other wine from vineyards within Château-Chalon must be labeled Côtes de Jura.)

"Château-Chalon is the grand cru of Vin Jaune. You don't have the right to produce Château-Chalon every vintage. A commission meets to decide whether to allow the appellation each year," explains Jean-François Bourdy, who has strong views about the roles of the varieties. "The tradition here—for more than fifty years—is that Chardonnay makes the best white wines. Savagnin makes Vin Jaune."

Emphasizing the expensive nature of its production, Vin Jaune is sold in an unusual 62 cl. bottle (supposedly to represent what is left after evaporation of a liter of wine from the harvest). Vin Jaune has an intensity that matches a top fino Sherry, but has a slightly different aroma and flavor spectrum, if anything deeper and more savory.

It would be a mistake to regard the difference between the traditional and ouillé styles as a polarizing influence: they are more the extremes of a continuum. Modernism is perhaps defined by Ganevat, who at the southern tip of the Jura is almost completely devoted to the ouillé style; his Chardonnays show a minerality and freshness reminiscent of Chablis. At the center are producers like Stéphane Tissot, making wines in both styles, but with oxidized wines varying from relatively brief exposure to the full reign of Vin Jaune. Traditional producer Jacques Puffeney made a Chardonnay in a style that shows herbs and spices of the garrigue with

26

Grape Varieties of the Jura

White

Chardonnay has a relatively lean style, more like Chablis than Côte d'Or, sometimes with savory impressions like Savagnin.

Savagnin is a nonaromatic variant of Gewürztraminer that makes wines with a savory character, whether in modern (nonoxidized or *ouillé*) style or traditional (oxidized or *sous voile*). The sole grape of vin jaune.

Black

Pinot Noir has a lighter style than Burgundy, with a relatively lean fruit spectrum tending to red cherries.

Poulsard is the major black grape, but lightly colored so that wines are often only a bit darker than rosé. Light body as well as light color.Often blended with Troussea or Pinot Noir to add structure. Known as Ploussard around Pupillin.

Trousseau tends to rusticity as a monovarietal, deep color, high in acidity and alcohol. It's often blended with Poulsard. Under the name of Bastardo, some is grown in the Douro, also grown in Spain under this and other names.

a touch of fenugreek leading into a savory palate, but which is more of a halfway house between traditional and ouillé as it doesn't have the madeirized quality of Vin Jaune.

Some producers now make a halfway style, typically by blending Chardonnay produced under ouillé conditions with a smaller proportion of Savagnin produced under voile. There are different stories about the origins of this approach, but it seems to be an attempt to introduce the oxidative style in a more subtle manner.

Split between Pinot Noir and the local varieties Poulsard and Trousseau, the reds in the Jura are less interesting than the whites.. The main change in the past few decades is an increase in Pinot Noir from almost negligible to around a third of black plantings. (However, Pinot Noir is not a newcomer: in the eighteenth century it was the second most planted variety.) Poulsard (also called Plousard locally) is by far the most important, representing more than three quarters of the black plantings (roughly a quarter of all plantings).

Poulsard and Trousseau are somewhat rustic in a light style. Poulsard has such a light, thin skin that it's often taken for rosé. It's relatively rare for Pinot Noir to acquire really enough concentration, although some of the wines from the glorious 2009 vintage could be mistaken for coming

Reference Wines for the Jura	
Chardonnay, ouillé	Domaine Ganevat, Les Chalasses
	Domaine du Pélican, Arbois
Savagnin, ouillé	Benedicte & Stéphane Tissot, Arbois (Traminer)
Chardonnay, tradi-tional	Domaine Macle, Côtes de Jura, Chardonnay Sous Voile
Savagnin, traditional	Benedicte & Stéphane Tissot, Arbois (Savagnin)
Trousseau	Chateau d'Arlay, Côtes du Jura, En Treize Vent
Vin Jaune	Domaine Berthet-Bondet, Château-Chalon
Vin de Paille	Domaine Jean Bourdy, Côtes de Jura

from the environs of Beaune. This might be an indication that the Jura would be a good place for Pinot Noir if global warming continues, although of course the presence of more clay and less limestone is problematic in that regard. I'm not sure I see much purpose in blending the varieties: it doesn't give Poulsard or Trousseau more refinement, nor does it round out Pinot Noir.

The wines of Jacques Puffeney were among the most subtle of the appellation, illustrating the differences between black varieties. The Pinot Noir is delicate but with a touch of austerity, somewhat in the direction of a red Sancerre, but tighter. Trousseau has more weight and depth, and although many Trousseau wines from the Jura can seem on the rustic side, Puffeney's Les Bérangères, with its slightly darker color and high alcohol, demonstrates the full potential of the variety for pulling off a richness that Pinot Noir cannot quite achieve in this environment. But Puffeney was recognized as the master of Trousseau before he retired.

A significant part of the Jura's production is Crémant, mostly made from Chardonnay, but some black grapes are also used. While there are exceptions, the Crémant is not usually especially interesting, and its main significance may be that it improves the quality of the still wines by using up grapes that are just short of full ripeness.

Even aside from its unique Vin Jaune, the Jura offers an unusual alternative to the monotony of simple fruit-driven wines; traditional or ouillé, Chardonnay or Savagnin, these are some of the more distinctive wines of France.

Savoie

It's hard to know what to expect of the wines of Savoie. Under the Alps, stretching from Grenoble to Geneva, it's far from obvious that this is a natural area for wine, yet production predates the Romans. Savoie became part of France only in 1860, so its grape varieties and traditions are distinct. Historically vines were planted all the way from the valleys up to around 1,000m of elevation. At the time of phylloxera, there were about 20,000 hectares of vineyards; since a recovery in the first two decades of the twentieth century, the planted area has been falling steadily, down today to little more than 2,000 ha. Almost all is in Savoie itself, with little left in Haut Savoie (Savoie is the southern half, and Haut Savoie is the northern half, of the former kingdom of Savoy, before it was annexed by France).

The most important vineyards are south of Chambéry, along the gorge of Chambéry or running along the Combe de Savoie, a striking 25-mile long valley bounded by the massive mountains that run on an axis from Chambéry through Aix-les-Bains and Annécy. On the gorge of Chambéry, Les Abymes and Apremont face the vineyards across the Combe de Savoie, where Saint-Jeoire-Prieuré, Chignin, Montmélian, Arbin and Cruet, face the mountains. Proximity to the mountains, and elevation of vineyards, make this distinctly cool climate territory, comparable to Alsace or the Loire.

Mont Granier looms over the vineyards of Chignin. Courtesy Savoie-Mont Blanc.

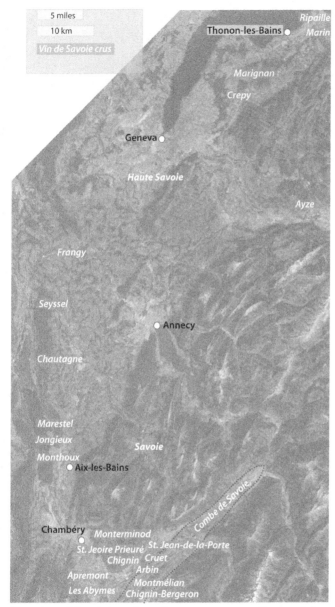

The wines of Savoie come from three separate areas: the remaining vineyards of Haut Savoie are near Lake Geneva; in the center are vineyards to the north of Aix-les-Bains; and the main group of vineyards is clustered to the south of Chambéry.

Most of the wine is white, and falls under the AOPs of Vin de Savoie or Roussette de Savoie (which is monovarietal Roussette from anywhere in the region). Roussette de Savoie has four crus that can be appended to

Grape Varieties of Savoie
White

Jacquère is the most important white grape of the region, typically cool-climate with high acidity. Can slip into herbaceousness. Sometimes blended with other varioeteis such as Chardonnay or Aligoté. Best consumed young.

Roussette is also known as Altesse, made as a monovarietal for AOP Roussette de Savoie, can also be blended in Vin de Savoie. High acidity, nutty character. Used for sparkling as well as still wines.

Roussanne is the great white grape of the Rhône, although not so refined in Savoie. Only ripens in the warmest sites. Known as Bergeron in the region.

Black

Gamay often uses carbonic maceration like Beaujolais, but is generally lighter.

Mondeuse is tannic and aromatic, can be astringent and peppery. It's related to Syrah. Usually monovarietal, but sometimes blended, e.g., with Gamay. High yields need to be controlled to avoid dilution. Carbonic maceration may be used.

Persan is a rare variety (thought extinct at one time), as a monovarietal is aromatic and structured.

its name: Frangy, Marestel, Monterminod, and Monthoux. The main difference in regulations is that yields must be lower in the Crus.

In addition to the 90% of production labeled as Vin de Savoie, there are fifteen crus, whose individual names can be appended to the Vin de Savoie AOP, which is really far too many separate appellations. The most important crus in terms of both quantity and reputation are Les Abymes and Apremont. There is a small amount of production under AOP Seyssel. There's also the IGP Allobrogies, which covers the whole area with a generally similar set of grape varieties. The fact, however, is that the variety, or the blend of varieties, is probably the most important factor in determining style.

Red wine is only a quarter of production, split between Gamay (probably introduced after phylloxera) and Mondeuse, an indigenous variety, with origins related to Syrah. Another indigenous variety called Persan is also found. Mondeuse is especially prominent in the Combe de Savoie, and notably in the crus Arbin and Saint-Jean-de-la-Porte. It gives a slightly astringent, peppery wine, quite tannic.

The best wines can be intriguingly different, and could hardly be more distinct from the modern "international" style, but sometimes lack flavor interest. The nutty notes of Jacquère at its best can be attractive;

Crus and Grape Varieties in Savoie

cru	white	red
Chambéry		
Apremont	100% Jacquère	
Les Abymes		
St-Jeoire-Prieuré	>80% Jacquère	
Chignin		>90% Gamay, Mondeuse, Pinot Noir
Chignin-Bergeron	100% Roussanne	
Combe de Savoie		
Montmélian	>80% Jacquère	
Cruet		
Arbin		100% Mondeuse
St-Jean-de-la-Porte		
Lac du Bourget		
Chautagne	>80% Jacquère	>90% Gamay, Mondeuse, Pinot Noir
Jongieux		
Haute Savoie		
Crépy	100% Chasselas	
Marignan		
Marin	>80% Chasselas	
Ripaille		
Ayze	>50% Gringet	
Savoie		
Roussette de Savoie	100% Altesse	

A blank space means the color is not permitted for the Cru.

the Roussanne of Chignin-Bergeron makes a fresher impression. The reds can be a bit rustic. Mondeuse is the most distinctive, but when very young it tends to show a fairly dull flavor spectrum, and it's hard for it to rise above the general level of rusticity, although Louis Magnin's top cuvées can become elegant with age.

Altogether there are 23 grape varieties in Savoie. The main white variety is Jacquère, which accounts for half of all plantings, and is supposed to have been imported into the region in the thirteenth century. It's a late-ripening, productive variety; in fact yields up to 78 hl/ha are allowed

32

Reference Wines for Savoie	
Roussette de Savoie	Domaine du Prieuré Saint Christophe
Vin de Savoie, Arbin	Domain Louis Magnin, Tout un Monde
Chignin-Bergeron	Domaine Louis Magnin, Grand Orgue

for the regional AOP, and between 65-75 hl/ha for the crus. Vins de Savoie are typically blends based on Jacquère; the major blending varieties are Chasselas, Roussanne, and Chardonnay. There are more specific assemblages in some of the crus. Les Abymes must be 80% Jacquère, and Apremont is exclusively Jacquère, as is Chignin; but Chignin-Bergeron is exclusively Roussanne. Crépy is exclusively Chasselas. (Crépy was a separate AOP until 2009, when it became a Cru of Vin de Savoie). The second most important white variety, Roussette, also known as Altesse, is mostly vinified as a monovarietal for the AOP Roussette de Savoie and its crus.

Vintages

Beaujolais

With almost all Beaujolais intended for immediate consumption, vintages are usually simply a guide as to whether or not to buy the current release. Even for the crus, little is available on the market beyond the last two or three years, but because there have been some unusually fine years lately, with exceptional potential for aging for the crus, there's more interest than usual. Recent ageworthy vintages were 2009, 2015, and the trio of 2018, 2019, and 2020. Very few wines are worth keeping more than a decade, however, and recommendations for longevity really apply only to the top crus, Moulin-à-Vent, Morgon, Fleurie, and perhaps Juliénas.

Vintage conditions have shown more extreme swings, with crops enormously reduced by hail in 2016 and 2017. "Normal years don't exist any more," says Jean-Louis Dutraive, whose vineyards were ravaged by a hailstorm both years. Two great vintages within a decade's span is unusual, but first 2009 and then 2015 produced wines with great generosity. "In all of Beaujolais, 2015 is a more southern style, but the grapes were ripe and there was good acidity and balance with potential to age," says Mee Godard. Is this a harbinger for the future resulting from climate change?

2021		Hail and frost reduced yield, cool wet conditions made for wines with fresh acidity. Wines are elegant but lighter than usual.
2020	**	Mild Spring, relatively dry hot summer, low yields gave wines with good concentration.
2019	***	Vintage is half the size of 2018 due to frost, summer heatwaves, and hail. Rain two weeks before harvest kept freshness; generally this is a fruit-forward vintage.
2018	***	The year did not start so well but changed at the end of June, after which there was continuously dry hot weather, with no rain before harvest, which was mostly in the first week of September. Because of the good water supply early in the season, although the wines are powerful, they have kept freshness and have lower alcohol than 2015. It's already regarded as potentially a legendary vintage.
2017	**	Hail storms and other climatic problems greatly reduced yields, but quality is very good. The top crus shows a mineral character and should age well.
2016	*	A restrained vintage, fresh from the Villages, tight from the Crus, but yields reduced by hail.
2015	***	A generous vintage, the richest and best rounded since 2009. Wines are ripe, round, and attractive. Some producers compare it to the legendary 1947.
2014		A cool August created problems but was followed by an Indian summer. However, many wines have rather high levels of acidity and appear a little tight rather than generous.
2013		A difficult vintage, with a cold wet start to the season, but good September. Fruits are light and pleasant, but the danger is that they will be overtaken by the acidity.
2012	**	"2012 is the smallest vintage I have experienced, with hail and rain early, but the weather became sunny from mid August. Harvest started from September 12; the quantity was not there but the quality was definitely there," says Georges Duboeuf.
2011	**	This is often considered to be as good as 2009, although it hasn't attracted the same attention; but the best wines will age well, as they have good concentration and structure.
2010	**	Another very good year, which would have been classic if not following 2009. There's a lot of fruit here, although not as opulent as 2009.
2009	***	"2009 is the best vintage I have known in my life. We had (all the) berries in perfect condition which I have never seen before," Georges Duboeuf said. The top crus will last for several years yet.

2008   A slow, late vintage that called for a lot of selection; wines were relatively short lived.

2007 * A nice vintage, small but with good quality.

2006   Rather a mixed vintage, generally with average results.

2005 *** A very good year, as in Burgundy; overshadowed in the decade only by 2009.

2004 * A normal vintage was a relief after the excessive heat of the previous year.

Visiting the Region

Beaujolais

There's essentially a village in each of the Crus, ranging in size from the small towns of Romanèche-Thorins or Villié-Morgon, to villages such as Fleurie or Saint-Amour, and hamlets like Juliénas. South of the Crus, there's no real center, except for Villefranche-sur-Saône, on the route from Mâcon to Lyon, east of the vineyards. Roads tend to twist and turn through the hills, so it's easy to get lost, which makes it sensible to allow plenty of time between appointments in different villages. While some producers have tasting rooms that are generally open, the region is less tourist-oriented than Côte d'Or, and it's a good idea to make appointments almost everywhere; the main risk with smaller producers is that, if you are not expected, everyone may be out in the vineyards.

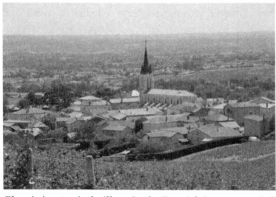

Fleurie is a typical village in the Beaujolais, surrounded by hills.

Some domains have an address that is only a zip code and a town name, sometimes with a lieu-dit added. Lieu-dits are mapped erratically, to say the least, in GPS devices in France, and the simplicity of the address does not necessarily mean the domain will be right

35

in the center of town, however, as the zip code may extend well beyond into the countryside. Ask for directions and allow extra time.

In several Beaujolais Crus, the Syndicat representing the producers has opened a boutique, where wines can be tasted, and purchased at the same price as at the domain. The boutiques are often more accessible—usually in a town center—and have more extended opening hours than the producers themselves (often including weekends). But remember that the lunch break is sacrosanct in France, so most tasting rooms are closed between 12:00 and 2 p.m. They make it possible to directly compare many wines (although the top producers are not necessarily represented); usually tasting is free. They include:

- Espace de Brouilly
  Parc de la Mairie, 69220 Saint Lager
  (+33 4 74 66 82 65) espace.brouilly@gmail.com
  www.espace-des-brouilly.com

- La Maison Du Cru Fleurie
  Rue des Crus, 69820 Fleurie,
  (+33 4 74 69 00 23) lamaisonducru@orange.fr
  www.maisonducrufleurie.fr

- Caveau de Cru Morgon
  56 Rue du Château Fontcrenne, 69910 Villié-Morgon
  (+33 4 74 04 20 99) contact@morgon.fr

- Caveau du Moulin-à-Vent
  1673 Le Moulin À Vent, 71570 Romanèche-Thorins
  (+33 3 85 35 58 09) union.moulinavent@orange.fr
  www.moulin-a-vent.net

- Caveau Du Cru Régnié
  298 Rue du Bourg, 69430 Régnié-Durette
  (+33 4 74 04 38 33) caveau@cru-regnie.fr
  caveau.cru-regnie.fr

- Caveau de Saint Amour
  Le Plâtre Durand, 71570 Saint-Amour-Bellevue
  (+33 3 85 37 15 98) tourisme@saint-amour-bellevue.fr
  www.saint-amour-bellevue.fr/st-amour-wine-cellar

The Jura

The Jura is more spread out than it seems, but most producers can be accessed from one of the two main towns, Château-Chalon and Arbois. In a really elevated position, Château-Chalon is one of the sights of the region in its own right. Arbois is a lively little town, with many producers

Arbois has a lively town center with many tasting rooms.

Chambéry is the capital of Savoie. Place St. Léger is the historic center.

represented by tasting rooms that are open all day. Don't be surprised to be offered red wines to taste before white, because the whites are so aromatic. "You won't be able to taste the reds after the Savagnin," is a common view.

Savoie

The heart of Savoie runs from the southern end of Lac du Bourget (around Aix-les-Bains) south to the main center of Chambéry, then turning to run along the edge of the mountains northeast to Albertville. It's quite dramatic terrain. Pierre Gaillard (of the northern Rhône) was instrumental in establishing a museum in Arbin, renovated in 2018-2019, which focuses on the grape varieties of the region:

- Musée de la Vigne and du Vin de Savoie
  46 rue Docteur Veyrat
  73800 Montmélian
  (+33 4 79 84 42 23) patrimoinemusee@montmelian.com
  montmelian.com/musee

Tasting

The etiquette of tasting assumes you will spit: producers will be surprised if you drink the wines. Tasting rooms usually have spittoons (crachoir in French). Of course, some tourists do enjoy drinking the wines, but producers will take you more seriously if you spit.

Profiles of Producers

Beaujolais	*42*
Jura	*99*
Savoie	*122*

Ratings

***	Excellent producers defining the very best of the appellation
**	Top producers whose wines typify the appellation
*	Very good producers making wines of character that rarely disappoint

Symbols for Producers

- Address
- Phone
- Owner/winemaker/contact
- @ Email
- Website
- Principal AOP or IGP
- Red White Reference wines
- Grower-producer
- Negociant (or purchases grapes)
- Conventional viticulture
- Sustainable viticulture
- Organic
- Biodynamic
- Natural Wine
- Wine with No Sulfur
- Vegan Wine

- Tasting room with especially warm welcome
- Tastings/visits possible
- By appointment only
- No visits
- Sales directly at producer
- No direct sales
- Winery with restaurant
- Winery with accommodation

ha=estate vineyards

bottles=annual production

Beaujolais

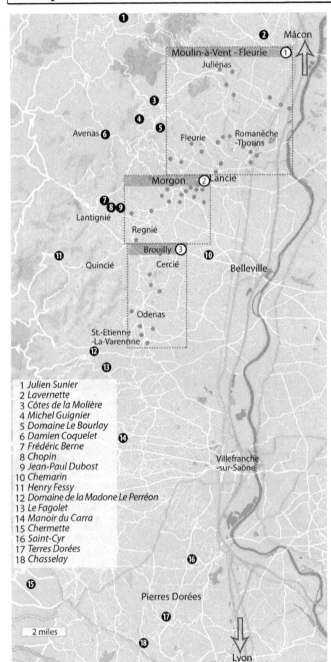

Moulin-à-Vent - Fleurie

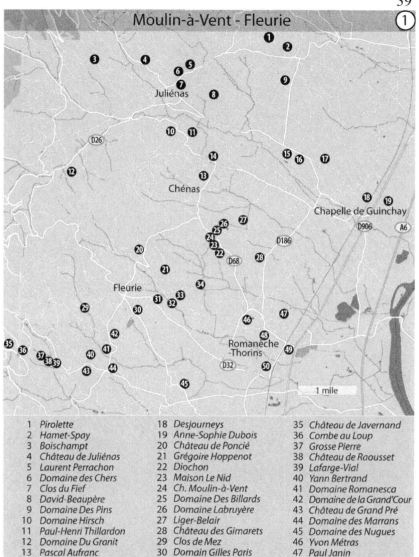

1 Pirolette	18 Desjourneys	35 Château de Javernand
2 Hamet-Spay	19 Anne-Sophie Dubois	36 Combe au Loup
3 Boischampt	20 Château de Poncié	37 Grosse Pierre
4 Château de Juliénas	21 Grégoire Hoppenot	38 Château de Raousset
5 Laurent Perrachon	22 Diochon	39 Lafarge-Vial
6 Domaine des Chers	23 Maison Le Nid	40 Yann Bertrand
7 Clos du Fief	24 Ch. Moulin-à-Vent	41 Domaine Romanesca
8 David-Beaupère	25 Domaine Des Billards	42 Domaine de la Grand'Cour
9 Domaine Des Pins	26 Domaine Labruyère	43 Château de Grand Pré
10 Domaine Hirsch	27 Liger-Belair	44 Domaine des Marrans
11 Paul-Henri Thillardon	28 Château des Gimarets	45 Domaine des Nugues
12 Domaine Du Granit	29 Clos de Mez	46 Yvon Métras
13 Pascal Aufranc	30 Domain Gilles Paris	47 Paul Janin
14 Chênepierre	31 Château des Bachelards	48 Richard Rottiers
15 Château Bonnet	32 Chignard	49 Ch. des Jacques
16 Domaine des Pierres	33 Métrat	50 Georges Duboeuf
17 Bel Avenir	34 Clos de la Roilette	

40

Morgon - Régnié-Durette

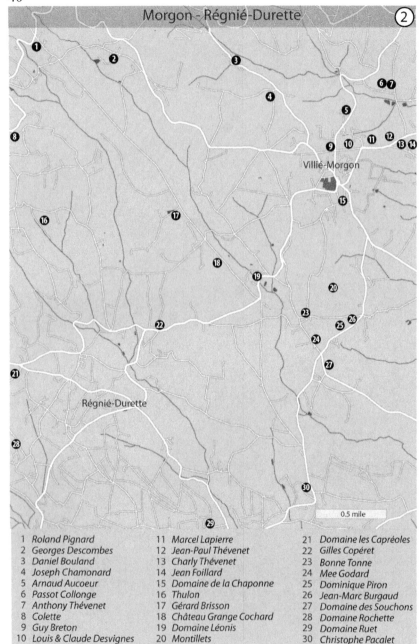

1 Roland Pignard	11 Marcel Lapierre	21 Domaine les Capréoles
2 Georges Descombes	12 Jean-Paul Thévenet	22 Gilles Copéret
3 Daniel Bouland	13 Charly Thévenet	23 Bonne Tonne
4 Joseph Chamonard	14 Jean Foillard	24 Mee Godard
5 Arnaud Aucoeur	15 Domaine de la Chaponne	25 Dominique Piron
6 Passot Collonge	16 Thulon	26 Jean-Marc Burgaud
7 Anthony Thévenet	17 Gérard Brisson	27 Domaine des Souchons
8 Colette	18 Château Grange Cochard	28 Domaine Rochette
9 Guy Breton	19 Domaine Léonis	29 Domaine Ruet
10 Louis & Claude Desvignes	20 Montillets	30 Christophe Pacalet

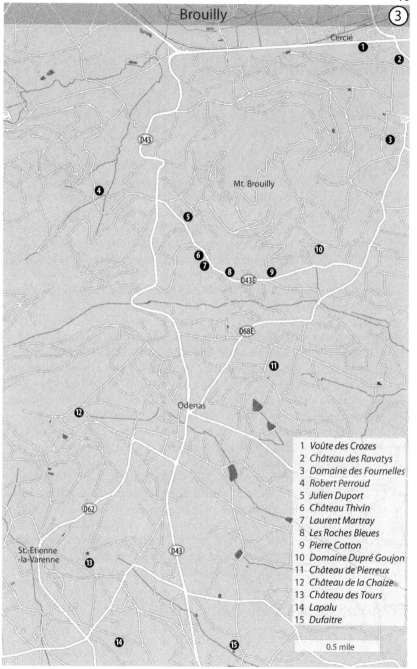

42

Profiles of Leading Estates

Domaine David-Beaupère *

69840 La Bottière, Juliénas	📞 +33 6 20 37 51 19
@ domaine.david.beaupere@gmail.com	👤 Louis-Clément David-Beaupère
🌐 www.domainedavidbeaupere.fr	🔴 Juliénas [map p. 39]
🗓 🏭 🍇 🌿 🍇 11 ha; 35,000 btl	🍷 Juliénas, La Bottière

LA CROIX
DE LA BOTTIÈRE
·•·
JULIÉNAS

Domaine David-Beaupère

A tasting here is not quite the usual experience. When we arrived, operatic choruses were coming out of the house. We could still hear the opera faintly in the tasting room. Louis-Clément explains that the family runs a music school. His grandfather bought the domain in the 1960s after returning from Algeria where he used to make wine. "My father was a doctor, and the vineyards were rented out. The renter retired in 2004 so I was able to take over 4 ha. I became organic almost straight away, and made my first vintage in 2008. I'm still the only organic producer in Juliénas."

Vineyards are mostly in Juliénas, with a large holding in the La Bottière *climat* near the winery. "In 2015 I took over another 4 ha, so I doubled the area all at once." This was 2 ha in La Vayolette (in Juliénas) and 2 ha in Moulin-à-Vent. "Vinification is semi- to almost full carbonic maceration. There's only one pump-over as the idea is to have carbonic maceration. Juliénas is a strong terroir—it can be rustic—at the beginning I started making wine with a lot of extract, but it means the wines have to be kept a long time, and I wanted to have something more immediate."

The Juliénas is the main cuvée, coming from young vines in La Bottière, but it will become a blend when La Vayolette is certified organic. It's aged only in tank. Silky and aromatic, it's intended for immediate enjoyment. The La Bottière cuvée comes from the oldest vines, around 70 years, with lower yields. It's also aged in tank. "Until 2014 I aged La Bottière in wood, but it's too much for the wine," Louis-Clément says. Longer maceration gives more presence on the palate, still in the style of carbonic maceration, with lovely aromatics against a silky background. La Vayolette comes from the classic blue rock terroir; a more powerful wine in the same style, it is soft, almost voluptuous. The domain offers an unusual opportunity to see different terroirs represented through the style of carbonic maceration.

Domaine du Clos du Fief *

49 Rue du Gamay, 69840 Juliénas	📞 +33 4 74 04 41 62
@ domaine@micheltete.com	👤 Michel & Sylvain Tête
🌐 www.micheltete.com	🔴 Juliénas [map p. 39]
🧑 🏭 🍇 🔄 17 ha; 80,000 btl	🍷 Juliénas, Cuvée Prestige

"It's been a family domain for four generations," says Françoise Tête. "When my husband, took over, it was only 6 ha. Michel expanded the domain, and since 2015, Sylvain has been working with his father, and he has added two new appellations, Chénas and Moulin-à-Vent." The label has changed from Michel Tête to Sylvain & Michel Tête.

The main focus is on local vineyards in Juliénas, which represent about half the domain. Most of the other half is Beaujolais Villages, which produces red, rosé, and white. The time that Michel Tête spent in Burgundy shows in his approach to winemaking, which ranges from traditional semi-carbonic maceration to completely Burgundian, depending on the cuvée.

Beaujolais Villages comes from close to Juliénas, on friable rocky soil. Made by semi-carbonic maceration, this is very much a modern Beaujolais, light, fruity, and tart. St. Amour gets a mixed approach, mostly semi-carbonic, but with 20% destemmed: it's rounder and softer than Beaujolais Villages, but follows the traditional Beaujolais style.

For Juliénas, there are three cuvées. Cuvée Tradition is all whole bunch (semi-carbonic) vinification in cement, and is aged entirely in cement; it's soft and approachable, with more presence than the St. Amour. Cuvée Prestige comes from three plots of old vines, aged from 80 to 100 years, with very small yields; aged half in cement and half in old tonneaux, there's more sense of structure, although still showing that soft, approachable, house style. Tête de Cuvée comes from a single parcel on terroir of blue rocks. It's 100% destemmed—"this is not the Beaujolais method, it's the Burgundian method," says Sylvain—and is vinified in a wooden cuve and then aged in tonneau of old wood. It shows more structure against that characteristic soft background. Very approachable for Juliénas, the wines are ready to drink on release.

Domaine Jules Desjourneys **

75 rue Jean Thorin Pontanevaux, 71570 La Chapelle de Guinchay	+33 3 85 23 11 10
@ contact@julesdesjourneys.fr	Fabien Duperray
www.julesdesjourneys.fr	Moulin-à-Vent [map p. 39]
7 ha; 20,000 btl	Fleurie, La Chapelle des Bois

Fabien Duperray started as a distributor, but when he acquired some very old vines in the Beaujolais crus in 2007, he switched to becoming a producer. "One day I was offered a parcel of Les Moriers that was as steep as Côte Rôtie and I couldn't resist—now it's my passion," Fabien says. Since then he has added other plots, and now produces several single vineyard cuvées, mostly from Fleurie and Moulin à Vent, as well as appellation wines. His vineyards are on the steepest slopes of the appellations, and are worked manually. Like any producer bringing quality to a region in difficulties, he has had problems with the authorities, and the 2008 l'Interdit

is from Fleurie but labeled Vin de France because it was refused the agrément to be labeled as an AOP wine.

There's no fixed mindset here: some years Fabien is first to pick, some years last. Winemaking is traditional, with whole clusters fermented for a month, malolactic fermentation delayed by cooling, and wines matured for 18 months in barrique. Production averages a few hundred cases for each of the single vineyard cuvées. The web site identifies the domain as located in "Bourgogne de Sud," but although the wines are often compared to the Côte de Nuits, they are not Beaujolais pretending to be Burgundy, but very much their own expression of Gamay. Helped by low yields from the old vines (some over 100-years-old), the sheer intensity of the fruits brings out Gamay's slightly higher-toned aromatics. Higher alcohol than usual for Beaujolais is a natural part of the style.

None of these are wines for instant gratification; all are serious wines requiring some aging. The typicity of each appellation really comes out, showing generosity for Fleurie and more reserve for Moulin à Vent. single-vineyard wines are more finely structured than the appellation wines; in fact the main difference is not the flavor spectrum but the level of refinement. Fabien started in Beaujolais, but then expanded into the Mâcon with cuvées from Mâcon-Verzé and Pouilly-Vinzelles.

Domaine Louis et Claude Desvignes *

135 rue de La Voute, 69910 Villié Morgon	☎ +33 4 74 04 23 35
@ louis.desvignes@orange.fr	👤 Louis-Benoît & Claude-Emmanuelle Desvignes
⊕ www.louis-claude-desvignes.com	Morgon [map p. 41]
11 ha; 50,000 btl	Morgon, Côte de Py

Devoted exclusively to Morgon, the domain is built around a courtyard just off one of the oldest streets in the village of Villié-Morgon. "We are at least the eighth generation, perhaps more because records were lost in the Revolution," says Louis-Benoît Desvignes. We had our tasting in an old cave. "This is the barrel cellar, but we don't use any barrels in my family, we think cement tanks are more interesting for what we are looking for. We have a lot of interesting flavors in the soils of Morgon, we want to preserve them. The wine is left alone in tank for 10 months or more with no racking until bottling," Louis-Benoît explains.

Depending on the vintage, there may be four or five cuvées, including the Côte du Py, where the Desvignes have 5 ha, half on the top of the hill and the rest in parcels lower down. A Vieilles Vignes cuvée comes from two small parcels of hundred-year-old vines on the hill. House style shows a linear purity to the fruits; some people might be inclined to call this minerality. The cuvées reflect their terroirs. The Vieilles Vignes has concentration as well as purity, and I might be inclined to place it in Moulin-à-Vent in a blind tasting or perhaps to think about Pommard. The Javernières, from a parcel in Côte du Py, has a softer impression than the Côte du Py itself: "They used to say 'Pinoté' to mean that some wines have a Burgundian character, and this is a very good example," says Louis-Benoît. Indeed, the subtlety of the cuvées is reminiscent of a tasting in Burgundy. All the wines come from estate grapes except for a small purchase of grapes for Morgon Corcelette.

Georges Duboeuf *

Hameau Duboeuf, 71570 Romanèche-Thorins	📞 +33 3 85 35 34 20
@ contact@duboeuf.com	👤 Franck Duboeuf
🌐 www.duboeuf.com	🍷 Moulin-à-Vent [map p. 39]
😊 🏭 🍇 🛢 🚜 50 ha; 30,000,000 btl	🍷 Fleurie, Rein de Gré

Duboeuf's headquarters at Romanèche-Thorins, on the eastern edge of the Beaujolais near Moulin-à-Vent, represent a vast enterprise, signposted as Hameau Duboeuf, with a museum, tasting room, bookshop, cafe, and all the facilities you could want. Signifying the discrepancy between Duboeuf and other producers, the vast winery occupies more than 6 ha—around the size of the average producer in Beaujolais.

Duboeuf produces Gamay everywhere it is grown in France, including Beaujolais, Mâconnais, Pays d'Oc, Côtes du Rhône, Ardèche, and Touraine. Famous for his tasting ability, Georges tasted every wine that is bottled. "I spend two hours tasting every day," he said. His son Franck took over in 2005, but Georges remained intimately involved until his death in 2020.

Duboeuf buys grapes and wine (with élevage at Duboeuf) from 300 growers and 20 cooperatives. The vast range extends from Nouveau, through Beaujolais and Beaujolais Villages, to the Crus. The Flower series is the best known, but there is an increasing number of individual cuvées indicated by the origin of the grower.

The model remains as it started, as a negociant buying grapes (for whites the grower presses the grapes and Duboeuf takes the must). The top line, Cuvée Prestige, is an assemblage of the best lots, depending on the year, but is available only in France. The house style (insofar as a style can be defined for such a wide range) is for open, forward fruits, giving a fresh impression on the palate with supple tannins in the background. The Fleurie is perhaps the epitome of this style.

The top wines on the international market all come from individual small domains. Pouilly Fuissé from Domaine Beranger comes from a 2 ha plot near the Roche de Solutré, with aging in 30% new barriques giving a powerful wine in the old style. Moving along the range of reds from Beaujolais Villages through the Crus, there is a continuous transition from the overt fruitiness of carbonic maceration to a more structured impression. Château de Saint Amour is just a fraction less obvious

46

than the Beaujolais Villages. Fleurie from the Clos des Quatre Vents follows the same trend, attractive but not weighty. The point at which structure begins to trump fruitiness comes in the Morgon of Domaine de Javernières, from the Côte du Py *climat*. Up to this point in the range, there is no aging in oak, so the change in character is intrinsic to each terroir. Château des Capitans is the only estate that Duboeuf actually owns in Beaujolais, and the Juliénas comes from the Capitans *climat*, of which Duboeuf owns a large share. This is the first wine in the series of Crus to have some destemming and some (20%) aging in barriques, and this is reflected in a greater smoothness. I've always thought this wine is one of the best from Juliénas. The Moulin à Vent from Domaine des Rosiers ages similarly, but the barriques are new, and it's structured enough that it usually needs an extra year before it's ready.

Domaine Jean Foillard ★★

38 Le Clachet, 69910 Villié Morgon	📞 +33 4 74 04 24 97
@ jean.foillard@wanadoo.fr	👤 Jean Foillard
	🔵 Morgon [map p. 41]
🔲 🌿 🍇 🛢 🍂 ⊘ 16 ha; 100,000 btl	🍷 Morgon, Corcelette

Morgon 2008
Appellation Morgon Contrôlée
" *Côte du Py* "
Mis en Bouteille par
Jean Foillard à 69910 Villié-Morgon
Product of France

One of the founder members of the "gang of four" who modernized Beaujolais, Jean Foillard took over his father's domain in 1980. The winery is an old farm that Jean and Agnes Foillard renovated, on the main road out of Villié-Morgon, close to the Côte du Py; it now also offers bed and breakfast for visitors. Alex Foillard joined his parents in 2016, and bought 2.5 ha in Brouilly and Côte de Brouilly from which he makes wine under his own label.

Most of the domain's vineyards are in Morgon, with the largest holding on Côte du Py. When Jean started, he had just 4 ha, mostly in Côte du Py and Corcelette (inherited from Agnes's parents). Today the largest holding is in Côte du Py. He used to buy grapes from Fleurie, but lost the supply after the storms of 2016 and 2017; he bought 3 ha in the Champagne lieu-dit in 2018. Beaujolais Nouveau (mostly exported to the United States and Canada) comes from a holding just outside Morgon. Winemaking is the same for all cuvées, using semi-carbonic maceration with no added sulfur. Jean ages his top cuvées in wood, but Alex uses a mix of vats and wood.

Alex's two cuvées show a reversal of the usual relationship between Brouilly and Côte de Brouilly. Perhaps because the vines on Côte de Brouilly are older (70 years) or on granite, whereas those in Brouilly are on sand and schist, the Côte de Brouilly is rounder with more weight and grip on the palate. The domain produces three cuvées from Morgon. Eponym is an assemblage from various plots (aged in vat). Corcelette, the lightest of the single-vineyard wines, comes from 80-year-old vines on sandstone, and matures in foudres; Côte du Py, by far Foillard's best known cuvée, comes from vines of varying age on schist and granite, and matures in barriques; and cuvée 3.14 (which carries a jazzy pi sign on the label, and has been made since 2003 only in the best vintages) comes from 100-year-old vines on the Côte du Py. Corcelette is the most approachable; Côte du Py and Fleurie really benefit from an extra couple of years after release. Foillard's wines have a lightness of touch that has sometimes led to comparisons with Chambolle Musigny (seen mostly clearly with Corcelette), and a classic sense of tension. The wines give a textbook illustration of the underlying terroirs: Corcelette is very fine, Côte du Py is well structured, and Fleurie is more generous.

Domaine Mee Godard   *

921 route de Morgon, 69910 Villié Morgon	☎ +33 6 66 47 00 64
@ domaine.meegodard@yahoo.fr	👤 Mee Godard
⊕ www.meegodard.com	◉ Morgon [map p. 41]
📋 🏭 🍇 🛢 🍂 8 ha; 35,000 btl	📍 Morgon, Grand Cras

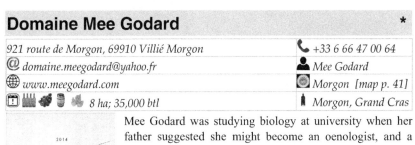

Mee Godard was studying biology at university when her father suggested she might become an oenologist, and a minor in wine science led her to Oregon and then back to France. Why Beaujolais? "Because I discovered these wines at a tasting in the region. When I left my winemaking job in Beaune, I came here to look for vineyards." At the end of 2012 she was able to buy in house in Morgon that came with 5 ha of vineyards. A year later she added another hectare in Moulin à Vent, and in 2017 another hectare. The average age of vines in the domain is 60-65 years (a 1 ha plot has 20-year-old vines). The house is just at the edge of Côte du Py. The domain is a work in progress, with the house slowly being renovated.

Mee's winemaking is distinctive. "I try to make vins de garde. I try to use as much whole bunch as possible, mostly about 70%, so there is some carbonic maceration, but I don't want to have a lot, just some in individual berries." Both punchdown and pumping-over are used. Everything is aged in wood, using a mixture of barriques, demi-muids, and foudres with only a little new wood. "Last year I didn't buy any new wood, the year before I bought a new demi-muid."

These are certainly wines for aging, quite reserved at first with a distinct tannic presence. Sometimes they have been criticized for having more structure than you expect from Beaujolais. They can be tight and austere with a touch of menthol turning medicinal in cooler vintages. There is certainly an impression of lots of extraction. Even rich vintages like 2015 give a strong sense of structure. The alcohol can be as high as 14% or more.

The 5 ha of Morgon are in three different climats, and each makes a separate cuvée. Corcelette tends to show red berry fruits with a touch of tannin at the end, Grand Cras is a little broader with just a touch more aromatic lift, and Côte du Py is the roundest and richest, but always with that sense of tension and precision waiting to emerge. There is also a barrel selection from a 1 ha plot in Côte du Py, called

Passerelle 557, which shows great purity of fruits. Fruits move from red towards black along the series. These are real wines expressing terroir but they need time to develop, at least two or three years after release; they prompt a comparison with Burgundy.

Domaine de la Grand'Cour   *

69820 La Grand'Cour, Fleurie	✆ +33 4 74 69 84 16
@ jlouis.dutraive@orange.fr	👤 Ophélie Dutraive
⊕ dutraive.jeanlouis.free.fr	Fleurie [map p. 39]
🚫 🍷 🍇 🛢 12 ha; 40,000 btl	Fleurie, Clos de la Grand'Cour

"My great grandfather bought our first vines, and we've been vignerons father to son for five generations," says Jean-Louis Dutraive. "We weren't in Fleurie at first, my father bought this domain in 1969." The winery is in the middle of the *clos* of Grand'Cour, which represents about half of the estate vineyards. A house is on one side of the courtyard, with winery buildings on the other side. There are vast cellars underneath. "At one point the domain was 20 ha and the facilities match, but my father only bought part of the vineyards," Jean-Louis explains. There are two labels. Domaine de la Grand'Cour is used for estate grapes. Jean Louis Dutraive is used to label wine made from purchased grapes.

"Vinification starts by putting grapes in a cold chamber at 6-7.5°C. Then we do nothing, not even temperature control. We don't want to extract too much, that's why we start at low temperature. The yeast are efficient even then, and temperatures don't go over 18°. We use barriques but usually some aging is done in stainless steel to maintain freshness." The mix varies with the cuvée, from equal proportions of all barriques, foudres, and stainless steel for the wine from the *clos*, to 100% barriques for the Vieilles Vignes.

Most of the vineyards are in large blocks close to the domain, and there are separate cuvées for each terroir. Two cuvées come from the Grand'Cour monopole surrounding the house: the Clos de la Grand'Cour, and the Vieilles Vignes, from vines about 70 years old. Outside of the Grand'Cour there are two terroirs in Fleurie, Champagne (immediately south of Grand'Cour) and Chapelle des Bois (the other side of the road). Because hail reduced the crop greatly in 2016, there was a Tous Ensemble bottling of Vieilles Vignes blended from all the holdings in Fleurie (it is very good).

The style of the Fleurie cuvées is fresh, emphasizing red fruits, elegant rather than fleshy, and is similar for the Jean-Louis Dutraive wines and the Grand'Cour estate, but Grand'Cour wines show more intensity. The Vieilles Vignes cuvée of Brouilly (from 50-year-old vines) is in the same style, perhaps a touch more four-square.

Domaine de la Grosse Pierre   *

409 Route de la Grosse Pierre, 69115 Chiroubles	+33 4 74 69 12 17
@ contact@lagrossepierre.fr	Pauline Passot
www.domainedelagrossepierre.fr	Chiroubles [map p. 39]
9 ha; 45,000 btl	Chiroubles, Claudius

Created by Georges Passot in the 1960s, the domain passed to his son Alain in 1979, and then Alain's daughter Pauline took over in 2018. Pauline was initially a sommelier at restaurant Pierre Orsi in Lyon before deciding that she wanted to take over the domain. "I traveled around to make wines in different places and came back here in 2018," she says. The domain is located in the middle of the hills of Chiroubles, along a narrow winding road at about 300m altitude (surrounding vineyards go up to 600m). It's very much a family affair: there's a residence at one end and a small winery at the other. Pauline's mother was running the bottling line when I visited.

Wines are vinified exclusively in concrete—"there is no wood, to keep the fruits, I want to show each terroir"—Pauline says. Vinification starts with semi-carbonic maceration, and after fermentation the wines age for 9-19 months. "I would like more time, but I don't have the space. "The core of the domain is in Chiroubles, with four cuvées, and there is also a cuvée from Fleurie, and one from Morgon. As you taste along the hierarchy, there is increasing sense of structure and more restraint to the fruits, The domain Chiroubles (from 3 ha all round the winery on deep soil on a granite base, facing east) shows fresh, lively fruits. Chiroubles cuvée Claudius (from a 1.5 ha plot of the oldest, 80-90-year vines, higher up the slope) is rounder and deeper in a similar style. Fleurie Bel-Air (from 50-year old vines in an 0.5 ha plot) is more 'serious,' adding structured herbal impressions to the fruits. Morgon Druby (from 70-year old vines in 0.8 ha) is more obviously structured and a little spicy. The surprise is Chiroubles aux Craz (from the highest vineyard at 480m on bedrock of granite, with mostly 70-year old vines) where restrained structure balances the juiciness of Chiroubles to give impressions of minerality. The top cuvée comes from the part of the famous Grille Midi lieu-dit that is in Chiroubles, and ages half in stainless steel and half in demi-muids.

Château des Jacques   ***

147 Les Jacques, 71570 Romanèche-Thorins	+33 3 85 35 51 64
@ contact@chateau-des-jacques.fr	Geneviève Bonifacio
www.chateau-des-jacques.fr	Moulin-à-Vent [map p. 39]
69 ha; 300,000 btl	Moulin-à-Vent, Clos du Grand Carquelin

For years, Château des Jacques, under the ownership of the Thorin family, produced a single wine that was the best in Moulin-à-Vent, quite Burgundian in its capacity to age. The estate was purchased by Burgundian negociant Louis Jadot in 1996, and then in 2001 Jadot extended the range by adding the Bellevue estate in Morgon, more or less doubling the size of the domain. There are 37 ha in Moulin-à-Vent, and 28 ha in Morgon. The wines are vinified following Burgundian practice (destemming and avoiding carbonic maceration) and spend several months maturing in barriques. A 9 ha plot of Chardonnay has been added, producing both Bourgogne Blanc and Beaujolais Blanc.

Château des Jacques occupies an extensive park on the outskirts of Romanèche Thorins; major renovations in 2017 constructed a new cuverie, and the existing buildings were completely renovated. The new cuverie is only for winemaking; wine will continue to be aged in the seventeenth century cellars underneath. "The idea is not to change the style, but to be able to make the wine more precise," said Cyril Chirouze, winemaker until he went to Clos Rougeard in the Loire in 2022. The cuverie has a mixture of stainless steel and concrete tanks. "Stainless steel tanks are used with pump-over when the berries are concentrated, but if we think more extraction is needed, we'll use concrete tanks with punch-down."

"The heart of our philosophy is to produce Gamay reflecting terroir like Pinot Noir does," Cyril explained. "We have two levels of wine: the blends, which I could compare with village wine in Burgundy; and then the single vineyards, which we could compare to premier crus." There is one blend each from Morgon, Fleurie, and Moulin-à-Vent. "Depending on the vintage we produce 7 different single-vineyard wines, 6 from Moulin-à-Vent and 1 from Morgon. You might think it is grand vin and second wine philosophy, but it is not at all that; we take the best barrels for the blends, and then if there is enough left over, we make the single-vineyard wines."

The wines have enough structure to require some time. The blends age with one third in tank and two thirds in barrique, and not much new oak. This showcases differences in terroir, a bit angular, uptight, and reserved for Morgon (you might say old-style for Morgon), fleshier for Fleurie, and broader with more sense of structure for Moulin-à-Vent. Single-vineyard wines have 20% new oak. Moulin-à-Vent cuvées show greater fruit concentration than the blends, with a sense of minerality you might describe as iron in the soil. Clos du Grand Carquelin may be the best representation of Gamay, showing the smooth, aromatic character that results when Gamay is treated as a serious variety. "Carquelin is only 50m from La Roche, but you will see it's different. It is probably one of the poorest soils you can find in France." Carquelin is a little rounder than La Roche, which comes from just below the windmill, and I really like its more Burgundian character—it reminds me of Pommard. Clos de Rochegrès has a sense of purity and minerality enhanced by its elevation at 360m. Champ de Cour is classically structured. Moving to Morgon, Côte du Py at almost the same elevation shows great sense of fruit purity and finesse. The wines drink well from about five years after the vintage to more than ten, and are a benchmark for the Burgundian style in Beaujolais.Château des Jacques also has 5 ha of Chardonnay which is used to make Beaujolais Blanc and Bourgogne Blanc. They are sold in different markets. The Beaujolais Blanc ages only in stainless steel. The Bourgogne Blanc ages in one third used barriques and two thirds stainless steel.

Domaine Paul Janin et Fils   **

651, rue de la Chanillière, 71570 Romanèche-Thorins	+33 3 85 35 52 80
@ contact@domaine-paul-janin.fr	Eric & Perrine Janin
www.domaine-paul-janin.fr	Moulin-à-Vent [map p. 39]
9 ha; 30,000 btl	Moulin-à-Vent, Vignes des Tremblay

"The history is very simple. Like many family domains it goes back to my great grandfather, who was a tonnelier and bought several parcels of vines. The domain has both increased and diminished. My grandfather rented some vineyards and bought some in an old lieu-dit, Tremblay, which became the name of the domain. My father rented some more parcels, and he was able to buy some of them later," explains Eric Janin, who came into the domain with his father in 1983, and took over when Paul retired in 2008. (Retired or not, Paul is still quite busy in the tasting room.)

Various labels are used, including Domaine des Vignes des Jumeaux for the Beaujolais Villages, or Domaine des Vignes du Tremblay, but the important thing to look for on the label is Paul Janin. Vinification is traditional, meaning mostly whole clusters for semi-carbonic maceration, with just a little destemming, and aging in stainless steel. Vinification and élevage are basically the same for all cuvées.

The domain is very much focused on Moulin-à-Vent, with just a hectare in Beaujolais Villages (both white and black). The wines are the quintessence of the style of maturation in cuve, emphasizing purity of black fruits, with tannins evident on the finish, but always supple. The Beaujolais Villages is quite restrained for the appellation, fresh and not too aromatic. There are three cuvées of Moulin-à-Vent. Vignes des Tremblay is an assemblage from several plots in the Tremblay lieu-dit (including some very old vines); it has that typical sense of purity and is very stylish. Heritage du Tremblay is an assemblage from plots of old vines, based on plantings by Eric's grandfather in the 1930s, with an average age over 90 years. Produced as a separate cuvée since 1991, this is the flagship of the domain. Les Greneriers is a single-vineyard wine, made as a separate cuvée since 2009, and coming from a 1 ha plot planted before 1914 and purchased in 1967, where very low yields give a great sense of purity. (It is matured in demi-muids.) There is greater concentration in the vieilles vignes and single-vineyard wines, but always that sense of purity and focus. The style carries over to the whites.

Domaine Jean-Claude Lapalu   *

979 Route de Moulin à Vent, Le petit Vernay, 69460 Saint Étienne La Varenne	☎ +33 4 74 03 50 57
@ jean-claudelapalu@wanadoo.fr	👤 Jean Claude Lapalu
	🔴 Brouilly [map v. 41]
🗓 🍇 🍷 🛢 🌿 ⊘ 8 ha; 80,000 btl	🍾 Brouilly, Vieilles Vignes

Jean-Claude takes Beaujolais to the extremes of late picking and high alcohol. Usually in Beaujolais an elevated alcohol level indicates chaptalization, but here it indicates extreme ripeness. In the 2009 vintage, some of the wines were labeled at 14.5% alcohol. (Levels came back down to 13% in 2011.) Viticulture is biodynamic, and yields are low, usually under 35 hl/ha.

Jean-Claude took over the domain from his father in 1996. Grapes had previously been sold to the cooperative, but Jean-Claude started making wine in 2000. His wines are unusual for Brouilly, which usually isn't particularly well distinguished from Beaujolais Villages, but here there is distinctly more structure.

Altogether there are six cuvées from eight separate parcels of vines, including two Vins de France, Beaujolais Villages Vieilles Vignes, Côte de Brouilly, and three cuvées from Brouilly. The named cuvées from Brouilly (Cuvée des Fous and Croix de Rameaux, which comes from a single parcel near the winery) are serious wines that may need a year or to resolve their tannins and come around. They are more like Morgon than the wines you usually find in Brouilly.

Vinification is traditional, but there is reduced use of carbonic maceration for Côte de Brouilly and Croix des Rameaux, which are matured in old barriques. There are experiments with maturing wine in amphora. The Alma Mater cuvée has full carbonic fermentation in concrete vats with whole clusters and ages for 7 months on skins in amphora. Winemaking follows natural precepts, including minimal use of sulfur, but the style makes a very rich impression. Some critics have described the style as "Beaujolais meets Priorat."

Domaine Marcel Lapierre   **

588 Rue Rabelais, 69910 Villié Morgon	☎ +33 4 74 04 23 89
@ informations@marcel-lapierre.com	👤 Mathieu & Camille Lapierre
🌐 www.marcel-lapierre.com	🔴 Morgon [map p. 41]
🗓 🍇 🍷 🛢 🌿 🍇 ⊘ 16 ha; 105,000 btl	🍾 Morgon

The name of Marcel Lapierre became a symbol of the revival of "serious" wine in the Beaujolais. The domain itself existed before the Revolution, but took its modern form after phylloxera under Marcel Lapierre's grandfather. It was among the first in the region to bottle its own wine. Marcel Lapierre initiated the move away from the image of Beaujolais as following semi-industrial techniques for making cheap and cheerful wine.

Located in the town of Villié-Morgon, the domain is divided into two separate sets of buildings; we tasted the wines in a courtyard surrounded by buildings constructed just after the Revolution. Today the domain is run by Mathieu Lapierre, who is continuing his father's focus on natural winemaking. The domain is completely in Morgon, but some of the production from young vines is declassified to Vin de France; "Young Gamay is very productive," explains Mathieu. When the year is sufficiently good there is a Vieilles Vignes bottling; this is the cuvée Marcel Lapierre.

Sulfur is always low, but some cuvées are bottled entirely without any. There's always a difference. "There's no rule, it depends on the vintage whether the wine with or without sulfur has more generosity," Mathieu says. My impression most often is that keeping sulfur down increases expression of fruit purity. Certainly the house style is towards a certain linear purity of fruits, quite tight and precise when young, and needing some time to open out.

Perhaps aided by warmer vintages, the style seems to have moved in a richer direction in recent years. Cuvées are divided by the age of vines, from the Raisins Gaulois (Vin de France), to the Morgon (60-year-old vines) or the Cuvée Camille (50-75-year-old-vines from the Côte de Py, first bottled separately in 2013), and the Cuvée Marcel (100-year-old vines (where the concentration of the old vines gives a richness that overcomes Morgon's usual restraint).

Yvon Métras ★★

La Pierre, 71570 Romanèche-Thorins	+33 3 85 35 59 82
+33 3 85 35 59 82	Yvon Métras
	Moulin-à-Vent [map p. 39]
6 ha; 17,000 btl	Fleurie, Vieilles Vignes

Yvon Métras is widely regarded as an honorary fifth member of the "gang of four" who brought fruit to Beaujolais by following the prescription of Jules Chauvet for more natural wine production. He has been making his own wines at the domain since leaving the cooperative in 1988. The official address is in Romanèche-Thorins, but the production facility is in Fleurie, just under the hill of the landmark church, La Madone, in the area of Grille-Midi.

Vineyards are broken up into many small parcels, and are farmed mostly manually on more or less organic principles, using a very old lightweight tractor. Winemaking uses carbonic maceration in cement cuves, and the wines are unmistakably "serious," with a sense of structure that carries them well past the usual superficial impression of Beaujolais. The entry-level cuvée is called Printemps, there are cuvées from both Fleurie and Moulin à Vent, and there has been a Vieilles Vignes from hundred-year-old vines from plots in Grille-Midi and La Madone in Fleurie. The Grille-Midi is the definitive cuvée from this lieu-dit—if you can find it.

54

Some people feel it blurs the line between Beaujolais and Burgundy. Ultime was based on selection from the very old vines, but has not been made since 2011.

The wines are well known in France, where they are something of a cult, but for years they were not exported to the United States because Yvon did not want to deal with the paperwork. In addition to helping his father, Yvon's son Jules has been making wine under his own name since 2015 at his father's facility, the first release being a Beaujolais Villages.

Château du Moulin-à-Vent   *

4 rue des Thorins, 71570 Romanèche-Thorins	📞 *+33 3 85 35 50 68*
@ *info@chateaudumoulinavent.com*	👤 *Brice Laffond*
🌐 *www.chateaudumoulinavent.com*	🔴 *Moulin-à-Vent [map p. 39]*
📅 🏭 🍇 🍷 *30 ha; 100,000 btl*	🍶 *Moulin à Vent*

The Château du Moulin-à-Vent (originally called the Château des Thorins) is located in the heart of appellation, 200m from the iconic eighteenth century-windmill that gave its name to the appellation. The château itself was rebuilt in the early nineteenth century, although the vaulted cellars underneath date from the sixteenth century. With vineyards at the center of the appellation, in many of the top *climats*, and many old vines, the domain should be a reference point. It was a perennial under-performer until it was purchased by Jean-Jacques Parinet and his son Edouard in 2009. An extensive program of renovation has replanted about a quarter of the vineyards and reorganized the cellars.

The estate produces only Moulin-à-Vent. It has 130 plots, some very small, in 23 of the appellation's 69 lieu-dits. Winemaking is not typical: " We don't do semi-carbonic maceration, only traditional vinification." Destemming may vary from 50-100% depending on the vintage. Most cuvées age in a mix of oak (barriques and 350-liter barrels, but no new oak) and stainless steel. The entry-level cuvée, Couvent de Thorins, comes from plots with more clay, and ages only in stainless steel "to showcase the fruits of Gamay." The estate wine is a blend for four plots around the château and the windmill, and is intended "to have more of a Moulin-à-Vent identity." It ages 20% in oak. There are three cuvées from specific lieu-dits, Les Vérillats (44 ha sandy terroir), Champ de Cour (3 ha of pebbly soils and limestone), and La Rochelle (4 ha facing south on granite). They age 30% in oak. The top of the range consists of two cuvées from single parcels, Grands Savarins from lieu-dit Aux Caves, and Clos de Londres in lieu-dit Moulin-à-Vent (from the *clos* adjacent to the château). They age in oak.

Couvent de Thorins is fresh and fruity. The general cuvee shows precision and elegance of fruits with a nicely delineated impression to the palate. Les Vérillats shows greater roundness and depth than the general cuvee, that extra weight bringing a more delicious quality to the palate. Champ de Cour has a sense of holding back on release and needs a little time for flavor variety to come out. La Rochelle has less immediately obvious fruits, more sense of structure, and needs a couple of years. The single parcel releases are vins de garde and may require several years to come around. Clos des Londres has a massive sense of structure, and may not be ready even after a few years.

Since 2016 the Parinets have also owned Domaine Roc des Boutires (see profile) in Pouilly-Fuissé, and the wine is made in Romanèche-Thorins.

Maison D. Piron *

1216 Route du Cru, 69910 Villié Morgon	+33 4 74 69 10 20
@ piron@maison-piron.fr	Julien Revillon
www.maison-piron.fr	Morgon [map p. 41]
25 ha; 700,000 btl	Morgon, Grand Cras

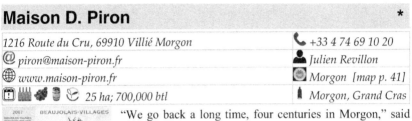

"We go back a long time, four centuries in Morgon," said Dominique Piron, whose domain occupies a group of buildings just below the Côte de Py. How many hectares do you have, I asked. "More and more, we are the principal producer in Beaujolais, mostly in Morgon, but also with a good diversity of other appellations. We have lots of small parcels. There are 15 cuvées, including 8 crus, with 4 cuvées in Morgon." Côte du Py was the first *climat* to be made as a separate cuvée, in 1996, and the others have followed. The Morgons all have different colors on the label to symbolize the different soils.

Do you use carbonic maceration? "Well what is that for you? It's really no more than using whole berries. For the crus we destem a large proportion of grapes because we want to bring out terroir. Our vinification is mostly traditional Burgundian with punch-down and pump-over. With Côte du Py or Moulin a Vent, for example, there are almost three weeks of maceration—we are looking for terroir." There is some élevage in wood only for the Morgons, a bit more for Côte du Py than the others.

"I don't know if you can talk of a style for the domain, each terroir is different, but we look for freshness and aromatic complexity, with a good balance. Many of the terroirs are calcareous with clay. When we get to granite, we look for delicacy. We'd rather have a wine that develops some complexity than one you can drink straight away in the modern style. Complexity does not come from vinification but from the soil."

Julien Revillon worked with Dominique from 2013 and took over the domain in 2020. Under Dominique, estate grapes were 90% of production, but now the balance has shifted towards purchased grapes. As well as moving production more in the direction of the negociant activity, Julien is focusing on producing cuvées from individual parcels in the Crus. The wines are quite sturdy. Beaujolais Blanc and Villages are light, fruity, and aromatic. Going to the crus, the wines become more serious, and with the cuvées from Morgon, the effects of long maceration are seen as tannic structure on the finish that requires a couple of years to integrate. Morgon La Chanaise is an assemblage from many plots. Showing that classic taut quality of granite, "it's very representative of the terroir of Morgon," Dominique says. Grand Cras comes from the south of the appellation, and is a little weightier. The top Morgon is, of course, Côte du Py, distinguished not so much by more power but by that typical combination of tautness and smoothness. Piron's top wine is probably the Chénas Quartz, which comes from an unusual parcel of 9 ha in Chénas where the granite is covered by Quartz crystals. It shows more generosity than the Morgon in the same general style.

Domaine Coudert Clos de La Roilette *

La Roilette, 69820 Fleurie	📞 +33 4 74 69 84 37
@ contact@laroilette.com	👤 Alain & Alexis Coudert
🌐 www.clos-de-la-roilette.com	🍇 Fleurie [map p. 39]
☺ 🏭 🍇 🛢 13 ha; 70,000 btl	🍾 Fleurie

The winery is located on a high point with views over the towns of Fleurie and Moulin-à-Vent. A workmanlike group of buildings is surrounded by vineyards; about half of the holdings are in the immediate vicinity, with the rest elsewhere in Fleurie except for 1 ha about 15 km away in Brouilly. Alain Coudert's father bought the domain in 1967, a small part of a 100 ha estate that was being sold. "We have a terroir that is a little different from the rest of the commune; it's granite but it's older and more decomposed. And when you get up to the border with Moulin-à-Vent, the soils have more clay and give more structured wine," Alain explains. (Before the appellations were created, some of the wine had actually been labeled as Moulin-à-Vent.) To get a more typical Fleurie Alain usually includes lots from the other holdings.

There are usually three cuvées of Fleurie: Clos de Roilette is an assemblage, Cuvée Tardive is a Vieilles Vignes, coming from 80-year-old vines close to the winery (tardive indicates that the wine is intended for aging), and Griffe de Marquis comes from the same vines as Cuvée Tardive, but is matured in barriques of 6-year wood for one year. Cuvée Christal, made in some years, is the antithesis of Tardive: made from young vines for early drinking. Vinification is traditional (using semi carbonic maceration). The house style is relatively sturdy: the wines are firmer than usual for Fleurie, and, at least when young, do not have that open fleshiness.

Domaine des Souchons *

Morgon, 69910 Villié Morgon	📞 +33 4 74 69 54 49
@ contact@1752.fr	👤 Quentin Brice
🌐 www.1752signaturewines.com	🍇 Morgon [map p. 41]
🚫 🏭 🍇 🛢 🍷 12 ha; 80,000 btl	🍾 Morgon, Cuvée Claude Pillet

The domain has been in the family since 1752 and has vineyards in 47 parcels scattered all over the Morgon appellation. The winery is in a functional group of buildings on the main road outside Villié Morgon. They describe the domain as "resolutely Morgon." "We vinify separately and blend at assemblage," says Baptiste Condemine, who started to modernize things when he came into the estate in 2008. "We should have more cuvées, my father did one, I do two, we should have five. We understand all the different *climats* of Morgon." In addition to the estate wines coming from Morgon, a small negociant activity (SARL 1752) extends the range into the other crus as well as Beaujolais and Beaujolais Villages.

In Morgon, the general bottling is Cuvée Lys; this is on the light side (and is extended by a bottling under screwcap called cuvée Tradition that's overtly for current drinking). The second major cuvée is Claude Pillet, which Baptiste introduced in 2009, named for his grandfather. This is a Vieilles Vignes bottling, coming from vines that are more than a hundred years old at Javernières on the Côte du Py. "This is more like Burgundy style," Baptiste says. Vinification starts in concrete for one month, then the wine is pressed off into barrel before fermentation has finished; fermentation is followed by MLF, and then a third is racked off to barriques of new oak, and the rest is matured in cuve. From the 2012 vintage there is a new cuvée, matured entirely in barriques, from the Grand Cras terroir.

Julien Sunier **

750 chemin des Noisetiers, Avenas, 69430 Deux-Grosnes	+33 4 74 69 91 74
@ contact@julien-sunier.com	Julien Sunier
www.julien-sunier.com	Morgon [map p. 38]
9 ha; 60,000 btl	Fleurie

"Here we are, 750m high, and there are no vineyards," Julien says. "The vineyards stop at 600m." Well off the beaten track for Beaujolais, Julien has a house and winery in a spectacular setting high up in the hills above Avenas (a few miles northwest of the Beaujolais crus). Originally purchased as somewhere to live when Julien came to Beaujolais, at the end of a long single track leading off from the main road to Avenas, the house is a stylish conversion of an old cow shed, and there is a small practical winery opposite.

"My parents live in Dijon but my family is not in the wine business. I made wine for other people for twenty years, in France and Italy. I came to Beaujolais in 2003 to start a new winery for Mommessin. I came with a bad idea of Beaujolais—the nouveau idea—but I discovered Beaujolais quickly because I had to buy the grapes for several crus, and I decided to start a little domain on my own in 2007. I'm renting vineyards, and I may change them, but I'll settle the domain around the present size."

Winemaking is a mix of the traditional and modern. It starts with carbonic maceration with the grapes covered by a layer of carbon dioxide. Maceration varies. "Depending on the year, I will macerate from 2 days to 35 days. I don't look for extract, I won't do punch-down or pump-over. We have natural coolness because fermentation is outside at 700 m. So even when there is long maceration there is not too much extraction. I want the vintage to express itself." The crus are mostly aged in barriques, using only old wood, varying from 10-15 years. "I do not use any young oak. I like to keep the fruit fresh so we don't like to age too long, the average is 8 months, but we won't go over 12 months. When we put the wine in the barrel, it's still fermenting, and because I don't use any sulfur before bottling, it really has the lees." A fraction of each cru is usually matured in cuve to keep freshness. One feature of the style is that alcohol levels are moderate, usually 12.5% or even less.

Because hailstorms seriously reduced the crop two years running, Julien purchased grapes for his entry-level wine, a Vin de France called Wild Soul, which shows slightly spicy red fruits with just a touch of aromatics. It's declassified to Vin de France because of continuous problems getting the agrément for the AOP. "The people who do the agrément don't like my style, they like thermovinification. I'll play the game for the crus, but not for this." But Wild Soul is a real wine, quite a contrast with the high-toned aromatics of much Beaujolais Villages.

There is one cuvée from each of Julien's three crus. "I blend because I have very small plots in each of the three terroirs, and I think I gain complexity by blending." Regnié is smooth and silky, Fleurie is smooth and spicy with hints of Fleurie's fleshiness showing, and Morgon is taut, crisp, and precise. "This is my favorite cuvée," Julien says. Julien points out that when he was at Mommessin he found an old wine list showing that in the 1920s, the crus of Beaujolais priced the same as Chambolle Musigny, and although he doesn't say it, you feel that his aim is get back there.

Domaine des Terres Dorées   *

565 route d'Alix, 69380 Charnay	☎ +33 4 78 47 93 45
@ contact@terresdorees.fr	👤 Jean Paul Brun
	🔴 Beaujolais [map p. 38]
📅 🏭 🍇 🛢 🍷 47 ha; 300,000 btl	🍾 Fleurie

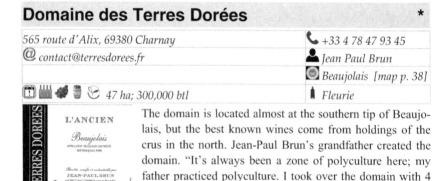

The domain is located almost at the southern tip of Beaujolais, but the best known wines come from holdings of the crus in the north. Jean-Paul Brun's grandfather created the domain. "It's always been a zone of polyculture here; my father practiced polyculture. I took over the domain with 4 ha and stopped the polyculture and started to plant white varieties, and then in the 1980s I planted Pinot Noir."

Today there are 9 ha of Chardonnay, 1 ha Roussanne, and 2.5 ha Pinot Noir; the rest is Gamay. The Chardonnay can be labeled as Beaujolais Blanc or Bourgogne, the Pinot Noir is Bourgogne AOP, and the Roussanne is a Vin de France. The Gamay includes 17 ha in crus, including Moulin-à-Vent, Fleurie, and Côte de Brouilly. Beaujolais l'Ancien comes from very old vines. The crus are managed by lutte raisonnée but in the south the domain is organic. Vinification is entirely conventional (with no semi carbonic maceration).

The house style shows serious wines, without any of the false aromatics that can pump up young Beaujolais and make it superficially attractive when young, but which don't really age in an interesting way. Jean-Paul's wines follow the Burgundian model, and even if Gamay mostly doesn't lend itself to making true Vins de Garde, they move in that direction. Jean-Paul has expanded his production into negociant territory: "To satisfy the demand from people looking for 'true Beaujolais'," he says. He also makes some late harvest botrytized wines.

Profiles of Important Estates

Vignoble Arnaud Aucoeur

Le Colombier, 135 Impasse du Colombier, 69910 Villié-Morgon	📞 *+33 4 74 04 16 89*
@ *arnaudaucoeur@vignobleaucoeur.com*	👤 *Arnaud Aucoeur*
🌐 *vignobleaucoeur.com*	🍷 *Morgon [map p. 41]*
🧍🏭🍇🚜	*12 ha*

The estate was established by the first Arcoeur in 1825; Arnold, who took over in 1998, is the tenth generation. Vineyards are quite spread out, with holdings in Morgon, Fleurie, Chiroubles, Juliénas, Saint-Amour, and Moulin-à-Vent, as well as Beaujolais Villages. There is also a negociant activity. There is one cuvée from the estate grapes for each Cru. The flagship is the Morgon, from 65-year-old vines planted by Arnold's grandfather. A Morgon Côte de Py comes from purchased grapes. Winemaking follows Burgundy. "We use punch-downs and pump-overs like Burgundy to give structure." There's been a move in recent years to use demi-muids for aging rather than foudres.

Pascal Aufranc

890 Chemin de Remont, 69840 Chénas	📞 *+33 6 85 05 59 37*
@ *pascal.aufranc@orange.fr*	👤 *Pascal Aufranc*
🌐 *www.pascal-aufranc.com*	🍷 *Chénas [map p. 39]*
📅🏭🍇🌿	*10 ha; 60,000 btl*

Pascal Aufranc describes his domain, located in the hills overlooking Chénas, as 'off the beaten track.' He does not come from a winemaking family, and started the domain, in an old stone house, with only a couple of hectares, surrounded by fields and woods. Vineyards are at 300m elevation, on sandy and granitic soil on the En Remont hill. Wine making follows semi-carbonic maceration in concrete vats, starting with whole clusters and then pressing off. The En Remont vineyard around the house has the oldest vines, and the cuvée is labeled Vignes de 1939. A second Chénas cuvée, Naturellement, has no added sulfur. The Chénas cuvées age for 8 months in concrete. Two Juliénas cuvées come from old vines, Les Cerisiers from a plot of 60-year old vines surrounded by cherry trees, and Probus from 70-year old vines. The two Juliénas cuvées see 25% aging in used barriques.

60

Château des Bachelards

69820 Fleurie	📞 *+33 4 74 04 10 42*
@ *visites@bachelards.com*	👤 *Alexandra de Vazeilles*
🌐 *www.bachelards.com*	🔴 *Fleurie [map p. 39]*
📅 🏭 🍇 🚜 🍷	*12 ha; 36,000 btl*

The domain takes its name from when the Benedictine monks of Cluny created an Abbey in 1100 and planted vineyards in a place they called Les Bachelards (The place of God in local dialect). The château is an elegant manor house that the monks built in the seventeenth century. The Platet family acquired the property during the French Revolution in 1793 and held it until 2007. (During the end of this period, Georges Duboeuf made a Fleurie from Château des Bachelards.) The property changed hands again in 2014 when Alexandra de Vazeilles bought the estate. Alexandra's background was as a consultant in the tech industry before she turned to viticulture and oenology. In 2022 she sold a majority share to an investor group that plans to convert the chateau into a luxury hotel; Alexandra continues to make the wine. By the time of purchase, vineyards were just a single block of 6 ha around the château, including a large proportion of old vines, with some dating from the first planting after phylloxera in 1910. There are another 2 ha in Fleurie at Lancié, 2 ha in Saint Amour, 1.25 ha in Moulin-à-Vent, and also 2 ha in IGP planted with Syrah and Viognier. Alexandra's objective is to make serious, ageworthy wines. "I don't like Beaujolais wines too much, that is why I created mine," she says. The difference is emphasized by bottling the wine in Bordeaux-shaped bottles. Winemaking starts with cold maceration with the grapes mostly (90%) destemmed, followed by conventional fermentation and aging. "We do not use any of the so-called 'Beaujolais winemaking methods'." Petite Fleur is an IGP aged in stainless steel. The Fleurie ages in a mix of stainless steel and foudres. Fleurie Le Clos comes specifically from the monks' old vineyard. The Saint Amour and Moulin-à-Vent age in a mix of foudres and 500-liter barrels, with 30% new oak. There's also some Pouilly Vinzelles from purchased grapes. The domain is into oenotourism and offers a variety of experiences in tours and tastings. These will be extended, as Alexandra sold a majority share in the property in 2022 to an investor who intends to create a hotel.

Domaine Bel Avenir

1087, Bel Avenir, 71570 La Chapelle de Guinchay	📞 *+33 6 12 63 32 42*
@ *domaine.bel.avenir@wanadoo.fr*	👤 *Cécile & Alain Dardanelli*
🌐 *www.domaine-bel-avenir.com*	🔴 *Moulin-à-Vent [map p. 39]*
📅 🏭 🍇 🌿	*19 ha; 70,000 btl*

The family's involvement with wine goes back three generations to Jean Dardanelli, who came from Italy to work in the Rhône. His son Albert moved to Beaujolais, and then in the next generation Alain Dardanelli, became one of the new wave of winemakers who are making more "serious" wines in Beaujolais. Alain took over the domain in 1986 and has focused on producing wines from the Crus, which now include Moulin-à-Vent, Morgon, Juliénas, Chénas, Régnié, and Saint-Amour. Vinification is conventional and the wines are aged in barriques. They are known for showing some power and potential to age.

Xavier Benier

1051 Route de la Croix du Bois, 69640 Saint-Julien	📞 *+33 6 62 60 65 17*
@ *xavier.benier@wanadoo.fr*	👤 *Xavier Benier*
🌐 *www.facebook.com/Xavier-Benier-1831854497078898*	*Beaujolais [map p. 38]*
🚫 🖌 🐛 🍂 🌿	*7 ha*

Xavier Benier comes from a family of vignerons, but after studying oenology in Beaune, started as a negociant in 1993. The family vineyards had been leased out, but he was able to take them over when the lease expired in 2001. The vineyards are in Beaujolais Villages, and remain the core of the estate in St. Julien (more or less where the granite area of the Crus makes the transition to the wider area of Beaujolais with sand and clay), supplemented by some other recent plantings nearby. Xavier also extends the range by buying grapes from Brouilly and Regnié. The main interest, however, is in the natural wine, usually made without added sulfur, never filtered. that comes from his own grapes. Cuvées include Nouveau and Beaujolais Villages. His attitude is typified when he asks, "What is the difference between my Beaujolais Nouveau and my regular Beaujolais?" and answers, "It's first of all a question of yields. With 70-year-old vines, I'm atypical, I get 42 hl/ha for Nouveau and 30 hl/ha for Beaujolais." These are very low yields by any measure. Describing the wine, Xavier says, "My primeur has a taste of very ripe fruit, cut by a touch of volatile acidity," going on to explain this is a feature of natural winemaking. Cuvée XB comes from 75-year old vines, some planted at the unusually high density of 12,000 /ha. The Vieilles Vignes cuvée comes from 100-year-old vines. The Beaujolais is made by semi-carbonic maceration. There's a Beaujolais Blanc, fermented and aged in tank (with the release of carbon dioxide blocked to eliminate the need to add sulfur). Not one to be bound by the appellation, Xavier has planted some Viognier, which is released as Vin de France.

Frédéric Berne

150 aux Vergers, 69430 Lantignié	📞 *+33 6 83 46 05 06*
@ *fredericberne69@hotmail.fr*	👤 *Frédéric Berne*
🌐 *www.fredericberne.com*	*Régnié [map p. 38]*
🧍 🏭 🐛 🍃	*12 ha; 30,000 btl*

Frédéric Berne comes from Beaujolais, although his family was involved in agriculture rather than winemaking. He established his own domain in 2014 at the Château des Vergers (an old estate, dating from 1604, which is owned by industrialist Pierre Henri Bassouls). Frédéric is committed to the commune of Lantignié, which he would like to see declared as the eleventh Cru of Beaujolais, with its terroir of pink granite and blue diorite stones. In addition to Beaujolais Villages from Lantignié (including cuvées Les Vergers and Pierre Bleue), there are Chiroubles (Les Terrasses) and Morgon (Corcelette). Vinification is by semi-carbonic maceration followed by aging in concrete for a few months.

Yann Bertrand

543 route du Château de Grand-pré, 69820 Fleurie	📞 *+33 4 74 69 81 96*
@ *lesbertrand.gp@gmail.com*	👤 *Yann Bertrand*

🌐 les-bertrand.com | 🔴 Fleurie [map p. 39]
| 8 ha; 48,000 btl

Guy and Annick Bertrand took over the family farm in 1992, and sold the wine in bulk. When Yann joined his parents in 2012, they started estate bottling. The estate holdings are 6.5 ha in Fleurie (in a single block known as the Grand Pré), 1.2 ha Morgon (with 60-year-old vines), and a hectare in Beaujolais, and grapes are purchased for a small additional production of Juliénas and Saint Amour. From Fleurie, Coup d'Folie comes from the youngest vines (anything under 50 years), Coup de Foudre comes from 2 ha of 60-year-old vines, Chaos comes from another 2 ha in two parcels of 45-70-year old vines, Emile is from a small block of very old vines, Chaos Suprême comes from the main block of 55-year-old vines, Grapes are fermented by carbonic maceration, and then the wine ages in a mix of barriques and demi-muids for 7-10 months.

Domaine Des Billards

Maison Jean Loron, 1846 Rn6, Pontanevaux, 71570 La Chapelle de Guinchay	📞 +33 3 85 36 81 20
@ vinloron@loron.fr	👤 Philippe Bardet
🌐 www.loron.fr	🔴 Moulin-à-Vent [map p. 39]
	9 ha; 72,000 btl

This is nominally a family-owned estate, in the same hands since the eighteenth century, but it is to all intents and purposes part of Maison Jean Loron, a negociant specializing in Beaujolais. Owned by Xavier and Nicolas Barbet, who are eighth generation descendants of the Jean Loron family, the domain is entirely in the lieu-dit Les Billards of St. Amour. Vinification is traditional semi-carbonic maceration, followed by aging in cement vat or oak foudres. Clos des Billards is a 1 ha vineyard that makes a separate cuvée.

Domaine de Boischampt

593 Rue des Vignes, 69840 Jullié	📞 +33 6 98 15 66 68
@ a.romero@domainedeboischampt.fr	👤 Antoine Romero
🌐 www.domainedeboischampt.fr	🔴 Juliénas [map p. 39]
	17 ha

This is actually an old estate, located in the main street of the village of Jullié, with vaulted cellars dating from the 16th century, but for years the product was sold off in bulk. Antoine Romero is a Burgundian who took over the domain. Winemaker Thibaud Baudin worked with Jean-Paul Brun in Beaujolais, spent a year working in New Zealand, and then returned to work at Domaine de la Vougeraie in Burgundy, and continued at Domaine d'Henri in Chablis. He took over as winemaker at Domaine de Boischampt in 2018. Production started with four cuvées from the domain and three from purchased grapes. The domain was called Maison de Boischampt until enough of the estate grapes came on line to provide all production, when the name changed to Domaine de Boischampt. With wines from four crus, this is a good opportunity to compare terroirs. Juliénas and Morgon age in stainless steel; Juliénas shows a smooth, elegant balance with quite a structured impression, while Morgon Les Charmes is tight and precise with the structure of Morgon. Fleurie and Saint Amour in 500-liter oak barrels; Fleurie makes a more generous, softer, rounder impression than Juliénas, but still shows some structure at the end; Saint Amour is softer and rounder, and more immediate, than Fleurie.

Domaine de la Bonne Tonne

1142 Montée du Py, Haut-Morgon, 69910 Villié Morgon	📞 *+33 6 12 54 31 62*
@ *domainedelabonnetonne@gmail.com*	👤 *Thomas & Anne-Laure Agatensi*
🌐 *bonnetonne.wordpress.com*	🔴 *Morgon [map p. 41]*
🚫 ⛭ 🍂 🍇 🍇	*7 ha; 35,000 btl*

The domain is located on the Côte de Py, the best *climat* in Morgan. Thomas Agatensi is the seventh generation of winemakers in the family, but effectively created the domain from his parents and in-laws holdings. Half the domain is in Morgon (spread over three *climats* of Grand Cras, Les Charmes, and Côte de Py), and in addition to the individual cuvées from each *climat*, there is a Vieilles Vignes cuvée from 90-year-old vines. The Morgon cuvées age in a mix of barriques and demi-muids. The domain was expanded with the most recent acquisition of 2.5 ha in Regnié, from which there are two cuvées: Agath'the Blues, aged partly in concrete and partly in demi-muids, and Cléa, which finishes fermentation and then ages in demi-muids. The Regnié cuvées are produced without any addition of sulfur. There are small holdings in Beaujolais, split between red and white.

Château Bonnet

2 les Paquelets, 71570 Chapelle Guinchay	📞 *+33 3 85 36 70 41*
@ *pierre-yves@chateau-bonnet.fr*	👤 *Pierre-Yves Perrachon*
🌐 *www.chateau-bonnet.fr*	🔴 *Moulin-à-Vent [map p. 39]*
🚶 ⛭ 🍂 🌿	*23 ha; 70,000 btl*

The actual château goes back to the seventeenth century, and the Perrachon family purchased it together with 7 ha of vineyards in the early nineteenth century. Pierre-Yves started working at Château Bonnet in 1985, and now his children, Charlotte and Julien, are involved. Although the château sits within Moulin à Vent, the major holding is 12 ha in Chénas, with another 3 ha each in Moulin à Vent, Juliénas, and Saint Amour. A small part of production is sold in bulk, but about three quarters is estate-bottled. Vinification takes a mixed approach, with about half the grapes destemmed (for conventional fermentation rather than semi-carbonic). There are three cuvées from Chénas, representing successively older vines. Le Clos comes from 45-year-old vines in the named lieu-dit (a monopole) and ages in foudre, 1054 comes from 70-year-old vines in Le Clos and En Pérelle, and then moves to barriques for malolactic fermentation and aging, and Confidence de l'Echevin comes from vines over 100 years old in Le Clos, aging for 12-15 months in used barriques. The Vieilles Vignes cuvées from Moulin à Vent and Juliénas come from 60-year-old vines and age for 12 months in concrete. The Vin de Garde cuvée of Moulin à Vent ages in barriques. Saint Amour, from the latest parcel, acquired in 2006 on Côte de Besset, ages in stainless steel. There are also entry-level wines fermented with semi-carbonic maceration, labeled as Chat'au Bonnet rouge, two whites, and a rosé.

64

Domaine Daniel Bouland

Corcelette, 69910 Villié Morgon	📞 *+33 4 74 69 14 71*
@ *bouland.daniel@free.fr*	👤 *Daniel Bouland*
🗓 🏭 🚜 *9 ha; 70,000 btl*	🔴 *Morgon [map p. 41]*

There are more than a few Boulands making wine in Morgon, but Daniel Bouland stands out from the crowd. Based in the hameau of Corcelette, he is known for his production of Morgons on the artisanal level—the domain represents his share of an inheritance after division of the family property—with very small scale production from the lieu-dits of Douby, Côte de Py and Delys. Many of the holdings are less than a hectare. This is essentially a one man operation. Vineyards are worked by hand: there isn't even a tractor. The Morgon Vieilles Vignes from Corcelette comes from ninety year old vines (planted in 1926). Some of the other plots are a mere forty or so years old. Vines are trimmed in the traditional closed gobelet, with no green harvest, because pruning ensures that yields are moderate. When vines die, they are replaced by selection massale from the vineyard. In addition to the Morgons, there are cuvées from Côte de Brouilly and Chiroubles. The Chiroubles is matured in cuve, but even so belies the reputation of the appellation as one of the lightest crus; the others are matured in old foudres. The word most often used to describe the Bouland wines is "traditional," meaning that they hark back to a much earlier era, with a more deeply colored, tannic style, and potential for development. Daniel recommends waiting five years before opening, after which they will age for several years. Comparisons are sometimes drawn with Burgundy.

Le Bourlay

Foretal, 69820 Vauxrenard	📞 *+33 6 72 15 17 37*
@ *le.bourlay@orange.fr*	👤 *Patrick & Odile Bourlay*
🌐 *www.lebourlay.fr*	🔴 *Beaujolais [map p. 38]*
🗓 🏭 📠 🍇 ☘	*10 ha*

The original vineyards of the domain are in Beaujolais Villages, but in the 1990s, the Bourlays expanded into Juliénas and then Brouilly. In the last decade they have diversified further by planting some new grape varieties, Pinot Noir and Chardonnay, but also Gamaret (a black variety created in Switzerland with Gamay as one parent), and Marsanne (the white variety from the Rhône). The wines are aged in the cellars of the medieval Chateau du Thil close by. The Beaujolais Villages is vinified by carbonic maceration, entirely in concrete. Brouilly comes from 70-year-old vines and is vinified one third by carbonic maceration and two thirds conventionally (from destemmed grapes). Juliénas is 50% destemmed, and ages in foudre.

Guy Breton

252 Rue Pasteur, 69910 Villié-Morgon	📞 *+33 4 74 69 12 67*
📠 *+33 4 74 04 21 13*	👤 *Guy Breton*
🚫 📏 🍇 🚜 🍾 *3 ha; 30,000 btl*	🔴 *Morgon [map p. 41]*

The estate sold its grapes to the coop until Guy Breton took over in 1986, and together with the other members of the "Gang of Four," (Marcel Lapierre, Jean-Paul Thévenet, and Jean Foillard) turned to an artisanal style of production. Half the domain lies in Mor-

65

gon, with additional plots in Regnié, Chiroubles, and Côte de Brouilly. After semi-carbonic maceration, wines are aged in three-year or older barriques. The top wine is the Morgon Vieilles Vignes, which comes from a hectare of 80-year old wines.

Gérard Brisson

240 Voie Romaine, 69910 Villié Morgon	📞 +33 4 74 04 21 60
@ vin.brisson@wanadoo.fr	👤 Louis Brisson
🌐 www.gerard-brisson.com	🔴 Morgon [map p. 41]
🚶 🏭 🍇 🍷	10 ha; 50,000 btl

This family domain was created when Michel Brisson returned from Algeria and bought an abandoned estate in 1958. His son Gérard took over joined in 1974, and from 2020 his son Louis has been in charge. Vines have an average age of 50 years, with the oldest planted in 1920. The heart of the domain is in the three cuvées from Morgon. "We use the traditional Morgon method—no thermovinification," they say. A blend from plots in the Charmes climat, La Louve is the original cuvée of the domain; fermentation starts with whole bunches and continues with pump-over and punch-down. It ages for 12 months in cuve. Vieilles Vignes come from the oldest vines, and ages in foudre for 12-18 months. The icon is Noble Tradition, which ages in barriques for 9-18 months. Beaujolais Villages comes from the Regnié area, and ages in cement cuve for 6 months.

Jean-Marc Burgaud

Morgon - La Côte du Py, 69910 Villié Morgon	📞 +33 4 74 69 16 10
@ burgaud@jean-marc-burgaud.com	👤 Jean-Marc Burgaud
🌐 www.jean-marc-burgaud.com	🔴 Morgon [map p. 41]
🏠 🏭 🍇 🍷	19 ha; 90,000 btl

Jean-Marc Burgaud and his wife Christine both come from grape-growing families, and they created their domain when they got married in 1989. Most of the vineyards are in Morgon, with several plots totaling 8 ha on the Côte du Py; there's one small plot in Regnié, and the rest are Beaujolais Villages. Vinification is the traditional semi-carbonic maceration; wines age in cuve, except for the Côte du Py, where some oak is used. Morgon Les Charmes and Grand Cras come from lieu-dits and age in cuve. There are several cuvées from the Côte du Py: the main cuvée ages in a mix of cuve and barriques, the Réserve ages in barriques, Javernières comes from a lieu-dit and ages in barriques, and James comes from the very top of the hill, also aged in barriques.

Domaine Joseph Burrier

Château de Beauregard, 71960 Fuissé	📞 +33 3 85 35 60 76
@ relation@joseph-burrier.fr	👤 Fréderic-Marc Burrier
🌐 www.joseph-burrier.com	🔴 Fleurie
🏠 🏭 🍇 🍂	5 ha; 20,000 btl

Frédéric-Marc Burrier expanded from Château de Beauregard (see profile in *Guide to Southern Burgundy*) in Pouilly-Fuissé by buying 5 ha in Beaujolais in 2007. He had previously bought plots in Fleurie and Moulin à Vent, and those are labeled as Château de

Beauregard. The wines from Juliénas, Saint Amour, and Chiroubles are labeled as Domaine Joseph Burrier. All the reds are made at the winery in Poncié (in Fleurie). Winemaking is a mix between traditional (semi-carbonic maceration) and Burgundian. "I have a problem in understanding semi-carbonic maceration, but of course we have some because we have 50% whole bunches that go into the tank underneath the 50% destemmed grapes. I do punch-down and pump-over daily. My objective is to produce reds in the same way as my colleagues in the north [in Burgundy]," Frédéric-Marc says. Aging uses a mix of barriques and foudres, and wines are bottled in November or December of the year following harvest. They have an unusual elegance for Beaujolais; Juliénas has a sense of precision that's unusual for the Cru, Fleurie is fruity but with a nice sense of precision, and Moulin à Vent shows a fine minerality. By way of experimentation, Frédéric-Marc planted some Syrah in Fleurie (0.15 ha just at the border with Moulin à Vent) and makes a varietal IGP Comtés Rhodaniennes called Granitik: it tastes very much as though it comes from the Northern Rhône.

Domaine les Capréoles

108, Impasse du Muguet, La Plaigne, 69430 Régnié-Durette	*+33 4 74 65 57 83*
contact@capreoles.com	*Cédric Lecareux*
www.capreoles.com	*Régnié [map p. 41]*
	8 ha; 35,000 btl

Cédric Lecareux was technical director at the large house of Gérard Bertrand in the Languedoc before buying 3 ha of an abandoned estate to start his own domain in Beaujolais, where his wife Catherine comes from. Capréoles is an old French word meaning vine tendrils. Cédric's rule is that there are no rules. So destemming and élevage may change with the vintage. Cuvée Cossenelle is a rosé, labeled as Vin de France. The range of reds starts with the Beaujolais Villages l'Amourgandise, labeled Terroir de Lantignié. There are three cuvées from Regnié. Chamodère is a blend of lots vinified by semi-carbonic maceration with lots that are destemmed for conventional fermentation. Diaclase is named for the granite subsoil and comes from the oldest parcels. Sous La Croix comes from the shallowest soils on top of granite. Diaclase and Sous La Croix age in barriques. L'Hydrophone comes from Brouilly, and is the only cuvée for which some grapes are purchased (from an organic grower).

Château de La Chaize

La Chaize, 69460 Odenas	*+33 4 74 03 41 05*
chateaudelachaize@wanadoo.fr	*Boris Gruy*
www.chateaudelachaize.fr	*Brouilly [map p. 41]*
	65 ha; 250,000 btl

Classified as a historic monument, built in the late eighteenth century, the château and its extensive gardens are a major tourist attraction. The domain was in the hands of the same aristocratic family for three hundred years, until it was sold in 2017 to Maïa Group, a real estate company. The winery and gardens are temporarily closed while a major restoration project is under way. The estate extends over 250 ha, and the vineyards are in a single block, although they are so large this extends over 11 separately defined lieu-dits. The wines represent almost 10% of the production of Brouilly, and have had a reputation for being easy-going, except for the Vieilles Vignes and Réserve de la Marquise, which have been more "serious."

Joseph Chamonard

585 chemin de la Grenouille, 69910 Villié Morgon	☎ *+33 4 74 69 13 97*
@ *g.chanudet@wanadoo.fr*	👤 *Genevieve Chanudet*
⊕ *domaine-chamonard.business.site*	⬤ *Morgon [map p. 41]*
📅 🏭 🍇 🥄	*6 ha; 35,000 btl*

Joseph Chamonard was one of the first growers to follow the artisanal approach of Jules Chauvet in his vineyards in Morgon; Chamonard was sometimes considered to be an additional member of the Gang of Four (Lapierre, Thévenet, Foillard, Breton). After he died in 1990, his daughter Genevieve and son-in-law Jean-Claude Chanudet took over the estate. Vineyards are spread around Morgon, with vines aged from 60-90 years. Grapes are picked late for maximum ripeness, vinification is by semi-carbonic maceration, and wines age in old foudres. In 2021 the domain added some parcels in Fleurie and Morgan and introduced a new cuvée, Fleurie Droit de Véto, a 'natural' wine with very low sulfur. The top wine is Le Clos de Lys, a blend from parcels in Les Martillets, Chenes and Corcelette.

Domaine de la Chaponne

70 Montée des Gaudets, 69910 Villié Morgon	☎ *+33 4 74 69 15 73*
@ *domaine-chaponne@wanadoo.fr*	👤 *Laurence & Laurent Guillet*
⊕ *www.laurent-guillet.com*	⬤ *Morgon [map p. 41]*
🏃 🏭 🍇 🚜	*14 ha*

Laurent Guillet and his wife Laurence took over the family estate in Morgon in 1987. In 2000 they acquired more old vines in Côte du Py, bringing the total to 12 ha in Morgon, with vines mostly around 60-years old. In 2009 they started to produce Chiroubles from the vineyards in Laurence's family. Much of the wine from Morgon is sold to Georges Duboeuf for his cuvée, Domaine de la Chaponne; restaurateur Georges Blanc also offers a Morgon Domaine de la Chaponne. Laurent bottles two cuvées from Morgon under his own label: the Cuvée Joseph blend and the Côte du Py lieu-dit.

Domaine Chasselay

127 chemin de la Roche. 69380 Châtillon d'Azergues	☎ *+33 6 83 88 55 45*
@ *contact@domaine-chasselay.com*	👤 *Claire Chasselay*
⊕ *www.domaine-chasselay.com*	⬤ *Beaujolais [map p. 38]*
📅 🏭 🍇 🥄 ⊘	*15 ha; 100,000 btl*

Located in the area of the Pierre Dorées, only about ten miles north of Lyon, the Chasselay family have been in the village since the fifteenth century. Jean-Gilles is a well-known figure in Beaujolais and made the transition in the 1980s into estate-bottling from selling wine to negociants. His children Claire and Fabien took over in 2008. The bulk of production goes into the Beaujolais nouveau and Beaujolais cuvées. Beaujolais Quatre Saisons is made by semi-carbonic maceration, but for other cuvées most grapes are de-

68

stemmed, there is punch-down to increase structure, and wines are aged in wood. Beaujolais Les Grands Eparcieux is a half-way house, aged in foudres. The Beaujolais Cuvée de la Platière is treated like the Crus: 80% destemmed, and aged in barriques for 12 months. The domain has plots in Brouilly and Côte de Brouilly, and extends the range of Crus by purchasing grapes from Chénas, Morgon, Fleurie, and Moulin à Vent. There are also Beaujolais Blanc, from a hectare of 35-year-old Chardonnay, aged in barriques, and a Pinot Noir from a small plot on clay-limestone soils.

Nicolas Chemarin

Les Villiers, 69430 Marchampt	📞 *+33 4 74 69 02 19*
@ *ptitgrobis@gmail.com*	👤 *Nicolas Chemarin*
📅 🏭 🍇 🖐 🍇 *8 ha; 30,000 btl*	🔴 *Beaujolais Villages [map p. 38]*

A bit off the beaten track, Nicolas Chemarin is located in Marchampt, at the base of the Beaujolais Vert mountains to the west. With vineyards at elevations from 450-600m on steep slopes (35-55%), exposed to the north wind, temperatures here are about 3°C cooler than, say, Fleurie. While this might have been marginal in the past, in the era of global warming it may be an advantage. Nicolas worked in the Loire, came back to Beaujolais in 2008, started by working some of the family vineyards and renting some more, and then in 2015 took over from his father, Lucien. Le P'tit Grobis is the basic Beaujolais Villages (there is also a white). Most is bottled at the domain but some is sold to negociants. Les Vignes de Jeannot is an unfiltered cuvée from 60-80-year-old vines, and is produced in the best years. Le Rocher is an unusual cuvée, coming from the highest plots. It's an illustration of the change in approach since Nicolas took over. His father tried to blend its distinctive character away, but Nicolas bottles it separately to show off the purity of fruits and minerality. The top cuvées come from small plots in Regnié and Morgon. All the wines are made by semi-carbonic maceration, except for Morgon Les Charmes and Vignes de Jeannot, where 80% of the grapes are destemmed. The Regnié and the Morgon Charmes age in a mixture of cement tanks and barriques, but Corcelettes from Morgon ages only in barriques.

Domaine de Chênepierre

Les Deschamps, 616 Route des Michauds, 69840 Chénas	📞 *+33 6 68 68 63 86*
@ *lapierre-christophe@wanadoo.fr*	👤 *Christophe Lapierre*
🌐 *www.christophe-lapierre.fr*	🔴 *Chénas [map p. 39]*
🚶 🏭 🍇 🌣	*11 ha; 25,000 btl*

Charles Lapierre created this small domain in 1924 with three parcels in Moulin à Vent. His son Gérard took over in 1960 and extended the domain into Chénas. The next generation, Christophe, took over in 2008. About half the crop is bottled at the estate, the rest going to the cooperative. All the reds have about 20% destemming and ferment in stainless steel with délestage (rack-and-return) and pumping-over. From Chénas there is a regular cuvée and a Vieilles Vignes from 50-year-old vines. Both Chénas cuvées and the Moulin à Vent Tradition age in foudre. The Moulin à Vent Fûts de Chêne ages in barriques for 10 months, and the Cuvée Prestige ages in barriques for 24 months. Christophe added a small parcel of Chardonnay to make Beaujolais Villages Blanc, which ages on its lees in cuve for 6 months.

Domaines Chermette

775 route du Vissoux, 69620 Saint Vérand	📞 +33 4 74 71 79 42
@ info@chermette.fr	👤 Pierre-Marie, Martine Jean-Etienne Chermette
🌐 www.chermette.fr	🔵 Beaujolais Villages [map p. 38]
📦 🏭 🍇 🛢 ✍	42 ha; 400,000 btl

Domaine du Vissoux is the original name of the property, where Pierre-Marie Chermette started estate bottling when he took over in 1982. Expansion since then led to the creation of Domaines Chermette (although the label usually says Pierre-Marie Chermette). Around the domain at the southern end of the appellation, the vineyards are simple Beaujolais, but there are also parcels farther north in Beaujolais Villages, and in Brouilly, Fleurie (plots of 4.5 and 2.7 ha in Poncié), and Moulin à Vent (three plots between 1 and 2 ha in La Rochelle). The original estate had 15 ha in Beaujolais, but now there are another 20 ha altogether in the Crus. Wines are fermented by semi-carbonic maceration— "we use this method because it is perfectly adapted to Gamay and to our terroir"—and aged in very old foudres, which were built by Pierre-Marie's grandfather. One Pierre-Marie's first wines, the Cuvée Traditionnelle, released in 1986 in a Burgundy-shaped bottle, created a stir for its emphasis on terroir: this is now the Origine Vieilles Vignes cuvée. Coeur de Vendanges is Beaujolais Villages, but comes from 100-year old vines on granite, and is regarded as approaching the Crus in character. Estate grapes are supplemented by a small amount of purchased grapes.

Domaine des Chers

Les Chers, 69840 Juliénas	📞 +33 6 75 54 61 40
@ contact@domaine-des-chers.fr	👤 Arnaud Briday
🌐 www.vins-arnaud-briday.com	🔵 Juliénas [map p. 39]
📦 🏭 🍇 🚜	5 ha; 50,000 btl

The small domain has passed from father to son for three generations. Vineyards include 4.5 ha in Juliénas, 4.5 ha in Saint Amour, and 1.5 ha in Moulin à Vent. In addition to the cuvées from each appellation, there are some single-vineyard wines: Le Secret de Mon Père from Juliénas, Arbre de Vie from Saint Amour, and Voyage dans le Temps from Moulain à Vent. The wines are all vinified by semi-carbonic maceration followed by aging in concrete.

Domaine Chignard

Le Point du Jour, 69820 Fleurie	📞 +33 4 74 04 11 87
@ contact@domaine-chignard.fr	👤 Cédric Chignard
🌐 domaine-chignard.fr	🔵 Fleurie [map p. 39]
🚶 🏭 🍇 🚜	10 ha; 45,000 btl

Under Michel Chignard, the domain became well known for its wine from Les Moriers, at the top of the hill just at the border of Fleurie with Moulin à Vent, where the granite soils also have some manganese, making a Fleurie with something of the structure of Moulin à Vent. During the 2000s, Michel gradually handed over to his son Cédric. who

70

took over in 2007 after spending time in Alsace and Australia. The vines are more than 60-years old; grapes are harvested manually, there is fermentation by semi-carbonic maceration in stainless steel or cement tanks, and then the wine is aged in old oak foudres. Recently some additional cuvées have been introduced. The Vieilles Vignes bottling has been renamed as Les Dix Coupées, and the new cuvée Le Cochonnier comes from two plots of really old (more than 100-year) vines. There is also now a cuvée, Beauvernay, from 60-year-old vines in Juliénas.

Domaine Raphaël Chopin

4 Chemin de la Savoye, 69430 Lantignié	📞 *+33 6 22 08 59 09*
@ *domaine.raphael.chopin@gmail.com*	👤 *Raphaël Chopin*
🌐 *www.domaine-raphael-chopin.fr*	🔘 *Régnié [map p. 38]*
🧍 🏭 🍇 🍂	*7 ha; 18,000 btl*

Raphaël Chopin made wine in Australia and then returned to Beaujolais in 2009 to take over the small estate of his grandfather. The vineyards include 1.5 ha of 65-year -old vines that make the La Savoye cuvée of Beaujolais Villages, 2 ha of 40-80-year-old vines in Regnié, and 1 ha of 60-year-old vines in Morgon Les Charmes. Vines range in age from the most recent plantings, which include some Chardonnay for Beaujolais Blanc, to the oldest dating from 1905. Fermentation is by carbonic maceration. There are several cuvées of Regnié from the largest plot. Le Ronze (the name of the lieu-dit) is the largest, Caprice comes from old vines in Laronze and ages for 12 months in 500-liter barrels, and Gaia comes from the oldest vines, aged for 6 months in a round concrete tank followed by 6 months in demi-muids. Morgon Archambault ages in barriques. Part of production is sold off to the negociants. The funky labels give an idea of the approach.

Clos de Mez

Raclets, 69820 Fleurie	📞 *+33 6 03 35 71 89*
@ *marie.elodie@closdemez.com*	👤 *Marie-Elodie Zighera*
🌐 *www.closdemez.com*	🔘 *Fleurie [map p. 39]*
📅 🏭 🍇 🍂	*5 ha; 20,000 btl*

Marie-Elodie Zighera is the fourth generation of women to own this family estate, and created the domain when she took over and left the coop in 2006 after obtaining degrees in viticulture and oenology. The name, MEZ, comes from her initials. Her aim is to "return to the wine of our ancestors." The model for winemaking is Burgundy. There are cuvées from Fleurie and Morgon, the style being dark and extracted for the "serious" wines Fleurie La Dot and Morgon Château Gaillard; Fleurie Mademoiselle M was introduced in 2015 as a lighter, easier-drinking style.

Domaine de Colette

4245 Route St Joseph, 69430 Lantignié	📞 *+33 4 74 69 25 73*
@ *domainedecolette@gmail.com*	👤 *Evelyne, Jacky, Pierre-Alexandre Gauthier*
🌐 *www.domainedecolette.com*	🔘 *Régnié [map p. 41]*
📅 🏭 🍇 🍂	*18 ha; 80,000 btl*

71

Jacky Gauthier started making wine in 1980, when he was only 17. He had planned to work with his parents, but an uncle offered to let him run a vineyard; in 1984 he bought that vineyard, and in 1994 he inherited his parents' vineyards and joined them into one estate. Today he works with his son Pierre-Alexandre. In addition to the original cuvées of Beaujolais Villages, Regnié, and Morgon, he has acquired plots in Fleurie and Moulin à Vent. The Beaujolais Villages, Beaujolais Villages Lantignié, and Regnié come from terroir of pink granite, (Lantignié has 55-year-old vines compared to Villages' 45 years), Fleurie comes from 50-year-old vines on granitic and alluvial soil, The Morgon comes from 80-year-old vines on schist in the Charme *climat*, and the Moulin à Vent comes from a 70-year old vineyard. All the wines except the Moulin à Vent are vinified by semi-carbonic maceration, followed by aging in concrete; the Moulin à Vent has 70% destemming for conventional fermentation.

Domaine de la Combe Au Loup

56 rue de la Bascule, 69115 Chiroubles	☎ +33 4 74 04 24 02
@ david.meziat@meziat.com	👤 David Méziat
⊕ www.meziat.com	◉ Chiroubles [map p. 39]
🏃 ⛏ 🍇 🗺	14 ha

The Méziat family have been making wine in Chiroubles since 1870. Albert Méziat was one of the first producers to start estate bottling, in the 1950s. His son Gérard built a winery in 1970, and formally created the domain in 1984. David, the next generation, joined the domain in 1993. Vineyards now include Chiroubles, Morgon, Régnié, and Beaujolais Villages, with a large proportion of old vines, having an average age of 50 years. There's some destemming before fermentation, and micro-oxygenation in tank, but no wood is used in aging as David believes it detracts from the purity of Beaujolais.

Gilles Copéret

1285 route des Chastys, 69430 Régnié-Durette	☎ +33 4 74 04 38 08
@ contact@domainegillescoperet.com	👤 Gilles Copéret
⊕ www.domainegillescoperet.com	◉ Régnié [map p. 41]
📅 ⛏ 📦 🍇 🗺	10 ha

Gilles Copéret started in 1986 with 2 ha in the area of Regnié from his maternal grandfather, Jean Trichard. In 1987 he retrieved some plots that had been leased out, with the grapes going to the cooperative. Since then the domain has grown further. When his wife Annie's parents retired in 1999, he obtained a hectare in Fleurie. In 2005, the Copérets constructed a new winery with modern equipment. The latest acquisition was 2.5 ha in Fleurie, which they had been leasing; this now makes the cuvée La Madone. Following the loss of the crop in Fleurie in 2016 and 2017 through storms, they added a small negociant activity, representing about 10% of production. Winemaking starts with semi-carbonic fermentation, and then follows with aging in concrete. Two typical cuvées from Regnié come from different areas, Les Chastys from around the winery, and Les Côtes from 60-year old vines in a plot facing northeast. Regnié Equation is described as a Cuvée d'Exception, with longer maceration, followed by aging in barriques (the only cuvée that ages in oak). All the Regnié cuvées come from granitic terroir, as does Fleurie La

72

Madone, where the soils are especially shallow. Morgon and Fleurie La Roche, by contrast, come from soils with more clay or sand.

Domaine Damien Coquelet

Les Bourrons, 69820 Vauxrenard	📞 +33 4 74 02 80 85
@ *damiencoquelet@hotmail.fr*	👤 *Damien Coquelet*
📅 🏭 🍇 ✋ *9 ha; 50,000 btl*	🌐 *Beaujolais [map p. 38]*

Damien Coquelet learned winemaking from his stepfather, Georges Descombes (see profile) and bottled his first vintage in 2007, when he was only 20. He now owns 2 ha and rents another 7 ha. He has 3 ha of Beaujolais and Beaujolais Villages, 2 ha of Chiroubles close to the domain, and 4 ha on Morgon's Côte du Py. He makes the wine at Georges Descombes. From Morgon he produces two cuvées; the major cuvée is produced traditionally in vat, but one third from plots at the very top of the hill is vinified in barriques for the Vieilles Vignes cuvée.

Les Côtes de la Molière

4 impasse du Charroi, 69820 Vauxrenard	📞 +33 6 85 04 50 09
@ *ibvins69@gmail.com*	👤 *Isabelle & Bruno Perraud*
🌐 *cotes-de-la-moliere.com*	🌐 *Beaujolais [map p. 38]*
📅 🏭 🍇 🍷 ✋ 🔲 🍇	*6 ha; 20,000 btl*

Isabelle and Bruno Perraud established the domain in 1987 with only 1.5 ha. It's grown since then by adding many small parcels. After Bruno suffered an adverse reaction to an insecticide, the domain became organic, and then biodynamic, and now practices natural winemaking, with little or no added sulfur. Grapes are purchased from organic growers to extend the range of wines under the negociant label of Maison B. Perraud. Côte de la Molière is made only in some years, from an 0.5 ha plot of 60-year-old vines in Moulin à Vent, but is labeled as Vin de France; after semi-carbonic maceration, it ages in old oak for 11 months. The Moulin à Vent comes from slightly younger (50-year) vines, and ages in a mix of stainless steel and oak. Le Poquelin is a Vin de France from sandy plots at 450m altitude in the area of Beaujolais Villages. The Maison Perraud range includes Saint-Véran, Pouilly Fuissé, Morgon, Fleurie, Brouilly, and Saint-Amour.

Bonnet Cotton

1369, Route Cote de Brouilly, 69460 Odenas	📞 +33 6 73 29 75 41
@ *bonnetcotton@outlook.fr*	👤 *Pierre Cotton & Marine Bonnet*
🌐 *Bonnet-Cotton.fr*	🌐 *Brouilly [map p. 41]*
📅 ▨ 🍇 ✋	*12 ha*

Pierre Cotton is essentially a new producer, although he comes from the Sanvers & Cotton domain, which has been making wine in Odenas since 1856. Pierre worked in the Loire before making his first cuvée in 2014 from 1 ha of Côte de Brouilly from the family vineyards. The following year he got 2 ha of Brouilly from the estate, and then purchased a hectare each of Regnié and Beaujolais. Pierre's father retired in 2017, so he then took over all the family holdings in Brouilly and Côte de Brouilly. All the cuvées are

73

made the same way, with fermentation by semi-carbonic maceration, and then the wines are aged in a mix of 80% foudres and 20% used barriques. The difference between the Pierre Cotton wines and those of the old Sanvers & Cotton domain is symbolized by the labels, jazzy and jokey for Pierre, conventional and plain for the domain.

Georges et Ghislaine Descombes

131 impasse du Puits Vermonts, 69910 Villié Morgon	📞 *+33 4 74 69 16 67*
@ *descombesgeorges@orange.fr*	👤 *Ghislaine Descombes*
🔲 🏭 🍇 🍇 *16 ha; 90,000 btl*	*Morgon [map p. 41]*

Georges took over his family estate in 1988. Half of the holdings are in Morgon, with other plots in Brouilly, Regnié, and Chiroubles, as well as Beaujolais Villages. Marcel Lapierre was his inspiration. Fermentation is by semi-carbonic maceration; wines age in old wood casks. Each Cru is divided into a regular cuvée and a Vieilles Vignes cuvée. The Morgon is quite reserved, with a good sense of structure when young. The winemaking approach is "natural," with minimal use of sulfur. In a break from Beaujolais, l'Orange is an orange wine, labeled as Vin de France.

Domaine Diochon

1198 Route Bourg, 71570 Romanèche-Thorins	📞 *+33 3 85 35 58 79*
@ *thomasestellepatenotre@wanadoo.fr*	👤 *Bernard Diochon*
🔲 📏 🍇 🚜 *5 ha*	*Moulin-à-Vent [map p. 39]*

The domain was founded in 1935, and Bernard took over from his father in 1967. Bernard retired in 2007; without family members to follow, he handed over to Thomas Patenôtre. The domain is just across the road from the famous windmill in Moulin à Vent and makes wine in the traditional way by semi-carbonic maceration. There are two cuvées: Tradition comes from 50-year old vines in the Champ du Cour by the winery and also in parcels close to Fleurie; the Vieilles Vignes comes from 100-year old vines in Champ du Cour. Tradition ages in old foudres and the Vieilles Vignes in old barriques. The wines have a following devoted to the traditional style.

Domaine Anne-Sophie Dubois

411 route des Rajats, Les Labourons, 69820 Fleurie	📞 *+33 4 74 69 84 45*
@ *asdubois69@gmail.com*	👤 *Anne-Sophie Dubois*
🌐 *anne-sophiedubois.blogspot.com*	*Fleurie [map p. 39]*
🔲 🏭 🍇 🍇	*8 ha; 35,000 btl*

Anne-Sophie Dubois comes from Champagne, and learned winemaking in Volnay, so it is not surprising that people find echoes of Burgundy in her wines. Ann-Sophie describes her methods as 'Burgundian in the manner of Henri Jayer', and there is no carbonic maceration here, except for the cuvée Les Cocottes. She makes four cuvées from an 8 ha parcel in Fleurie. The wines for immediate enjoyment are Les Cocottes and the Paso Doublé Gamay, a Bourgogne Rouge, that comes from the young vines, and is vinified like Burgundy, with complete destemming, traditional fermentation, followed by aging in demi-muids. The Fleurie cuvée l'Achemiste comes from 40-year old vines and is vinified

74

the same way, and ages half in cuve, half in 3-7-year old barrels ranging from 228 to 600-liter. The Clepsydre Fleurie, which has been renamed Les Labourons after the lieu-dit, comes from a parcel of 60-year-old vines planted at high (10,000/ha) density on granite, and ages exclusively in barriques.

Domaine Jean-Paul Dubost

166 Imp. du Tracot, 69430 Lantignié	📞 *+33 4 74 04 87 51*
@ *j.p-dubost@wanadoo.fr*	👤 *Jean-Paul Dubost*
🌐 *www.domainedubost.com*	🔴 *Régnié [map p. 38]*
🗓️🎨🍇🍂∅	*32 ha; 170,000 btl*

Originally known as Domaine du Tracot, the property was purchased by Henri Dubost in 1960. His son Jean-Paul, now runs the domain with his sons, Corentin and Joffrey. Half the domain is in the Crus, with include 6 ha in several *climats* of Morgon, 3-4 ha each in Moulin-à-Vent, Fleurie, Brouilly, and Régnié; the other half is in Beaujolais Villages (13 ha red and 3 ha white). All the cuvées from the Crus carry the names of specific *climats*. There are also cuvées from Moulin à Vent and Fleurie vinified without any addition of sulfur. Fermentation is by semi-carbonic maceration, Beaujolais Villages and Brouilly age in concrete, and the top cuvées from individual *climats* age in 400-liter barrels.

Laurence et Rémi Dufaitre

Domaine de Botheland, 69460 Saint Étienne des Oullières	📞 *+33 4 74 03 55 69*
@ *botheland@wanadoo.fr*	👤 *Rémi Dufaitre*
🗓️🏭🍇🍂∅ *15 ha; 50,000 btl*	🔴 *Beaujolais Villages [map p. 41]*

Rémi and his wife Laurence Dufaitre bought the Domaine de Botheland in 2006, in Beaujolais Villages just on the edge of Brouilly. Existing contracts required grapes to be sent to the cooperative, and they started producing wine in 2010. Once the obligation to the cooperative ended, the vineyards were converted to organic. Rémi is part of the natural wine movement: there is no chaptalization and no addition of sulfur (even at bottling, sulfur is zero or less than 2 mgm). They are followers of the group encouraged by Jules Chauvet, who use semi-carbonic maceration, with vinification essentially the same for all cuvées. In fact, before starting the domain, Rémi worked with Jean-Claude Lapalu, and made his first wines in Lapalu's cellars. The range runs from Beaujolais Nouveau and Beaujolais Villages to the crus of Brouilly, Côte de Brouilly, and Juliénas. (There's 1 ha of Chardonnay on sandier soils for Beaujolais Blanc.) Wines ferment and age in concrete tanks for six months, except for Côte de Brouilly which sees barriques. Côte de Brouilly stands out for coming from 80-year-old vines. Brouilly Boldness is a cuvée from a small, very steep plot where the grapes ripen a week later; it's been bottled separately from the Brouilly since 2016.

Julien Duport

56 Montée de la Chapelle, Brouilly, 69460 Odenas	📞 *+33 4 74 03 44 13*
@ *jul.duport@wanadoo.fr*	👤 *Julien Duport*
🚶🏭🍇🍂 *8 ha; 25,000 btl*	🔴 *Brouilly [map p. 41]*

75

The family has owned vineyards since 1916, and Julien took over 4.5 ha in 2003, when he was only 22; subsequently he added more vineyards from the family. Aside from some Beaujolais Villages just to the south, the vineyards are all in Brouilly and Côte de Brouilly. Julien also makes the wine at a neighboring domain, the Domaine des Cadoles. Fermentation is semi-carbonic—the objective is "more infusion than fermentation," Julien says—then the wines age in cuve with some use of barrels. There are several cuvées from different parcels, making a range of 8 wines. Côte-de-Brouilly Brouilly comes from lieu-dit Brouilly, Empreintes is based on a selection from various parcels, aged in tonneaux, and Boucheratte comes from a parcel of vines planted in 1885 (the first planting after phylloxera).

Domaine Dupré Goujon

404 Montée l'Écluse, 69220 Saint-Lager	📞 *+33 6 24 06 57 33*
@ *dupregoujon@gmail.com*	👤 *Guillaume Goujon*
🌐 *www.dupregoujon.fr*	🔴 *Brouilly [map p. 41]*
🗓 🏭 🍇 🥄	*16 ha; 60,000 btl*

Guillaume Goujon and Sébastien Dupré were childhood friends, from the Beaujolais, both interested in wine, who worked with Frédéric Pourtalie at Domaine de Montcalmès in the Languedoc, although not at the same time. They began to buy or rent parcels around the southern and eastern slopes of Mont Brouilly in 2013. They have plots in three terroirs, which they vinify individually. The Côte de Brouilly 6.3.1 is a blend from all three. From individual areas, La Pavé comes from the east, and L'Héronde comes from the south, both from plots on blue diorite rock. All three age for 12 months in a mix of barriques and demi-muids, followed by a period in vat. La Démarrante is a simpler cuvée, aged for just 6 months in concrete. There are also Beaujolais Villages in both red and white.

Domaine de Fa

Faye, 974 Route de Vers 71700 Boyer	📞 *+33 4 75 84 67 52*
@ *contact@domainegraillot.com*	👤 *Antoine & Maxime Graillot*
🚫 📏 🍇 🥄 ⬡ *8 ha; 35,000 btl*	🔴 *Saint Amour*

Brothers Maxime and Antoine Graillot run Domaine Alain Graillot (see profile in *Guide to Northern Rhône*) and in 2013 they extended their activities to Beaujolais. (The address of the domain is their mother's house near Tournon-sur-Rhône, a restored stone farmhouse where the wines are made.) First they bought a 5 ha vineyard on the Côte de Besset, high and rocky, overlooking the village of Saint Amour. Most of the vineyard is in Beaujolais, but 1 ha is in Saint Amour. Soils are on pink granite and granitic sand. The next year they bought another 3 ha in the Roche Guillon lieu-dit of Fleurie, at one of the highest points in the appellation, also on granite, but with some clay and limestone. They produce three cuvées. All ferment by semi-carbonic maceration in concrete. Beaujolais En Besset ages in cement and demi-muids. The Saint Amour comes from older (40-year) vines, the vines for the Roche Guillon Fleurie are 45-years old, and both age in 1-3-year-old foudre and some demi-muids.

76

Domaine Le Fagolet

2932 route d'Arbuissonnas, 69460 Vaux-en-Beaujolais	📞 +33 4 74 03 28 37
@ contact@le-fagolet.com	👤 Paul Girard
🌐 www.le-fagolet.com	Beaujolais Villages [map p. 38]
🗓 🏭 🍇 🚜 ⃠	10 ha

This family domain dates from 1850. Paul and Valérie Girard have been running the estate since 1980. The range starts with the Beaujolais Villages Granit series, in all three colors (the domain has a small planting of Chardonnay for white wine), including a red cuvée made with no added sulfur. A step up, Chai d'Oeuvre (in both red and white) comes from slopes with gradients over 30%. Granit ages in vat, Chai d'Oeuvre ages in oak. There are 4 Crus: Brouilly, Côtes de Brouilly, Chiroubles, and Morgon, which are vinified after destemming (that is, conventionally as opposed to the semi-carbonic maceration of the Beaujolais Villages). Brouilly cuvée Saburin Sud ages in oak. The domain is into oenotourism and offers a variety of experience from visiting the vineyards to tastings.

Henry Fessy

644 Route de Bel Air, 69220 Saint Jean d'Ardières	📞 +33 4 74 66 00 16
@ contact@henryfessy.com	👤 Laurent Chevalier
🌐 www.henryfessy.com	Beaujolais [map p. 38]
🗓 🎋 🍇 🛢 🚜	70 ha; 450,000 btl

The Fessy family ran this large local negociant in Brouilly from 1888 until 2008, when they sold it to the Louis Latour negociant in Beaune. It owns vineyards in all the Beaujolais Crus, and also in the Mâconnais, but the majority of production comes from purchased grapes. Louis Latour installed a new team and began a program of replanting the vineyards. In 2013 Henry Fessy took over the Château des Labourons, with 18 ha in Fleurie. The wines are workmanlike, but the best cuvées are from named vineyards, Château des Reyssiers in Regnié, and Château des Labourons in Fleurie. The marque Henry Fessy was dropped after 2022, and the wines are now labeled as Louis Latour.

Domaine des Fournelles

137 Montée de Godefroy, 69220 Saint Lager	📞 +33 6 79 17 27 53
@ domainedesfournelles@outlook.fr	👤 Guillaume Dumontet & Mariannick Bernillon.
🌐 www.domainedesfournelles.com	Brouilly [map p. 41]
🧍 🏭 🍇 ☺	8 ha; 30,000 btl

This small domain, which produces only Brouilly and Côte de Brouilly, is now in its third generation. François Bernillon established the domain in 147, his son Alain took over in 1973, and Alain's daughter Mariannick and her husband Guillaume took over in 2015. The Brouilly comes from 40-year-old vines and the Côte de Brouilly from 65-year-old vines. The Sans Artifice cuvée of Brouilly is made without sulfur and shows greater fruit purity than the conventional Brouilly. There are two special cuvées from Cote de

77

Brouilly: Godefroy comes from the lieu-dit of that name and shows extra weight; Elixir des Fournelles is based on selection of the best lots, and has some destemming for conventional vinification before aging in barriques for 8 months. It is more structured and needs some time before opening: this is a serious wine.

Château des Gimarets

1213b route de La Chapelle, 71570 Romanèche-Thorins	📞 *+33 6 80 08 23 05*
@ *contact@chateaudesgimarets.fr*	👤 *Éric & Nathalie Boyer*
🌐 *www.chateaudesgimarets.fr*	🔘 *Moulin-à-Vent [map p. 39]*
🔲 🏭 🏠 🍇 🚜 ◯ 🛇	*4 ha; 12,000 btl*

Château des Gimarets was built in the seventeenth century and reconstructed in 1810. The small château is situated in gracious gardens. Éric and Nathalie Boyer purchased the property in 2007, with a small vineyard surrounding the building, all in one block in the AOP of Moulin à Vent. The vineyard has a homogeneous terroir of pink granite rich in manganese, but there are several cuvées, distinguished by differences in winemaking. The line starts with Harmonie, Quintessence come from old vines, and is vinified conventionally from destemmed grapes, Céleste is vinified similarly but has no added sulfur, and Fût de Chêne ages in barriques. The wines all bear the same label of Château des Gimarets, with the individual cuvée indicated by a small sticker just above.

Domaine Château de Grand Pré

Grand Pré, 69820 Fleurie	📞 *+33 4 74 69 82 19*
@ *claude.zordan@infonie.fr*	👤 *Romain Zordan*
🌐 *domainegrandpre.com*	🔘 *Fleurie [map p. 39]*
🚶 🏭 🍇 🛠	*8 ha; 35,000 btl*

Louis and Renée Bertrand bought the domaine in 1972. Their children Guy and Christine (married to Claude Zordan) took over in due course, and then in 2012, grandson Romain Zordan took over half the estate, the other half going to his cousin Yann Bertrand, who works with his parents Guy and Annick under the domaine name of Les Bertrand. They share a cellar and tasting room. Romain worked with Ganevat in the Jura and has moved towards natural winemaking practices, with minimal use of sulfur and no filtration. Wines are made by semi-carbonic maceration, followed by aging in foudres or smaller barrels. The Fleurie comes from vines more than 30-years old, aged in a mixture of foudres and barrels Fleurie Cuvée Spaciale, from 60-60-year old vines, ferments in a spherical vat (made of fiberglass and called the Sputnik) and then ages in demi-muids, while Fleurie Vieilles Vignes ages in barriques. Morgon and Morgon Vieilles Vignes follow similar aging regimes. The Beaujolais AOP ages in concrete. The range is expanded a little by buying some grapes.

Château Grange Cochard

1562 voie Romaine, 69910 Villié Morgon	📞 *+33 6 60 21 46 76*
@ *contact@lagrangecochard.com*	👤 *Jean-Philippe Manchès*
🌐 *www.lagrangecochard.com*	🔘 *Morgon [map p. 41]*
🔲 🏭 🍇 🛠	*10 ha; 55,000 btl*

78

Jean-Philippe Manchès from Lyon, founded Maison Orcia, a wine trading company, in 2016, and then bought the domain from Sarah and James Wilding, who were not previously involved in making wine, and had bought the domain in 2008. It is located entirely in Morgon, including 1.5 ha on the Côte du Py. Most of the vineyards are close to the cellar; vines are old, between 40 and 100-years old. There are two styles of winemaking. For the major cuvée, the Vieilles Vignes, there is traditional semi-carbonic maceration, extended by using low temperature. The wine ages only in old foudres. Les Charmes uses a more Burgundian approach, with complete destemming leading to conventional fermentation; then the wine ages in barriques, including a little new oak. Côte du Py is the top wine, produced like Les Charmes. In top vintages, another cuvée, Côte du Py 1759, is fermented as well as aged in oak.

Domaine du Granit

226 route des Michauds, 69840 Chénas	📞 +33 6 80 59 35 46
@ fbessone@bbox.fr	👤 Franck Bessone
🌐 www.domaine-du-granit.com	🔘 Chénas [map p. 39]
🏃 🏭 🍇 �	12 ha

After qualifying in oenology, Franck Bessone took over the family estate, Domaine de la Croix Barraud, in Chénas. In 2005, he took over his in-law's estate, Domaine du Granit, with vineyards in Moulin à Vent. The range starts with Moulin à Vent Tradition, completely destemmed for conventional fermentation, and vinified entirely in concrete. Les Caves from 60-year-old vines and ages for 9 months in barriques; Lucile Maud comes from a 1 ha plot of 60-year-old vines and ages in barriques for 18 months; La Rochelle comes from 70-year-old vines and ages for 16 months in barriques. Other cuvées includes Fleurie, Chénas and Saint Amour, as well as Beaujolais Blanc and sparkling rosé.

Michel Guignier

40 impasse Faudon, 69820 Vauxrenard	📞 +33 4 74 69 91 52
@ earlguigniermichel@wanadoo.fr	👤 Michel Guignier
🌐 www.vignebioguignier.com	🔘 Morgon [map p. 38]
🗂 🏭 🍇 🚜 🔘 🍇 ⊘	4 ha; 20,000 btl

Practicing polyculture, with his small plots of vineyards surrounded by 30 ha of woods and fields rather than a monoculture, Michel Guignier has been committed to 'natural' winemaking since he established the estate in 1989 with 3 ha in Morgon AOP. Michel prefers to call the wines 'pure juice' rather than 'natural wines.' Vinification is by semi-carbonic maceration, followed by aging in vat for the first cuvées, and in barriques for the top cuvées. Several cuvées of 'natural' wines are Vin de France, even though they come from vines in the Crus, such as Moncailleux, from plots in Moulin à Vent. There are AOP wines from Beaujolais Villages, Fleurie, and Moulin à Vent. Amethystes is a negociant range of natural wines, at lower prices than the Guignier estate wines.

Domaine Hamet-Spay

Place de l'Eglise, 71570 Saint Amour Bellevue	📞 +33 6 61 71 67 66
@ info@hamet-spay.fr	👤 Christophe Spay

⊕ www.hamet-spay.fr ◉ Saint Amour [map p. 39]

18 ha; 110,000 btl

The family started winemaking in 1920, and Paul Spay established the Domaine de la Cave Lamartine in 1965, and in the next generation Christophe Spay and his sister Rachel Hamet extended it in 2005 into the Domaine Hamet-Spay. The focus is on Saint Amour, but there are also cuvées from Moulin à Vent and Juliénas, as well as a cuvée from Pouilly Fuissé, and Bourgogne Blanc. Beaujolais is vinified by semi-carbonic maceration and mostly aged in concrete.

Domaine Céline & Nicolas Hirsch

Lieu-dit Les Brureaux 345, route du Fief, 69840 Chénas	☎ +33 6 79 66 09 44
@ contact@domainehirsch.fr	👤 Céline & Nicolas Hirsch
⊕ www.domainehirsch.fr	◉ Chénas [map p. 39]
	5 ha; 30,000 btl

Céline and Nicolas Hirsch come from Alsace, and after qualifying in oenology and gaining experience, set up their own domain in Chénas in 2011. Their major holding is in Les Brureaux in Chénas, with old vines growing on a granite slope, but they also have plots in Moulin à Vent, Juliénas, and Beaujolais Villages. The domain is small enough that they can do everything themselves. The Beaujolais Villages, Juliénas, and Chénas are vinified by semi-carbonic maceration; Moulin Vent and the Les Brureaux cuvée from Chénas are 70% destemmed for conventional fermentation, and then age for 12 months in barriques.

Domaine Grégoire Hoppenot

Les Roches, 69820 Fleurie	☎ +33 7 85 60 02 01
@ greghoppenot@hotmail.com	👤 Grégoire Hoppenot
⊕ www.domainehoppenot.com	◉ Fleurie [map p. 39]
	10 ha; 50,000 btl

Grégoire Hoppenot was in charge of the cooperative Vignerons de Bel Air before working at Maison Trénel; and then Domaine du Vissoux, before he established his own domain in 2018 by buying the vineyards of Jean-Paul Champagnon. He has plots in several climats of Fleurie, Les Moriers (very close to Moulin à Vent), Les Garants, Poncié, La Roilette, Les Roches, and also in Morgon's Corcelette. All the cuvées ferment by semi-carbonic maceration in concrete. Fleurie Origines and Indigène age in vat, Morgon Corcelette in a mix of vat and barriques, Fleurie Clos de l'Amandier (from *climat* Poncié) and Les Moriers age in a mix of foudres and barriques.

Château de Javernand

421 impasse de Javernand, 69115 Chiroubles	☎ +33 9 63 29 82 13
@ chateau@javernand.com	👤 Arthur Fourneau & Pierre Prost
⊕ www.javernand.com	◉ Chiroubles [map p. 39]
	12 ha; 50,000 btl

80

This family domain was founded in 1917 and is now in its fifth generation. Arthur Fourneau and his cousin Mathilde Pénicaud, with her husband Philippe Prost, have been in charge since 2011. They have expanded the range since they took over. Vineyards are in two areas: 10 ha at Chiroubles are in an estate of 60 ha; and 3 ha in Mâcon came from the Prost family. Most production is accounted for by the original two cuvées from Chiroubles, Les Gatilles (vinified by semi-carbonic maceration), and the Vieilles Vignes (vinified by a mix of semi-carbonic maceration and conventional fermentation). Indigène is a smaller production of a 'natural' wine with no added sulfur. All these age in concrete. Climax is the latest cuvée, aged in barriques. From Mâcon there are white Mâcon Villages and red Mâcon Pinot Noir, and also a Bourgogne Chardonnay.

Château de Juliénas

Lieu-Dit Le Château, 337 Route de Vaux, 69840 Juliénas	📞 +33 6 73 83 03 11
@ tourisme@chateaudejulienas.com	👤 Thierry Condemine & Anita Berger
🌐 www.chateaudejulienas.com	◉ Juliénas [map p. 39]
🧍 🏭 🍇 🍂	40 ha; 25,000 btl

The château dates from 1582, although it was constructed in its present form in 1740. It claims to have the longest cellar in Beaujolais (350m), with vaulted ceilings of local stone. Thierry Condemine's great grandfather bought and restored the château in 1907. Vineyards includes the largest individual holding in Juliénas, and plots in Fleurie and Moulin à Vent. The domain describes itself as 'one of the pillars of oenotourism in Beaujolais,' and offers tastings and picnics in the grounds. From Juliénas, Cuvée Bessy ferments by semi-carbonic maceration and ages in stainless steel, Tradition and Cuvée Prestige and partially destemmed for conventional fermentation and age in very old foudres, and Le Clos ages in a recent foudre. Fleurie ages in old foudre and Moulin à Vent ages in barriques.

Domaine Labruyère

310 rue des Thorins 71570, Romanèche-Thorins	📞 +33 3 85 20 38 13
@ info@labruyere.wine	👤 Édouard Labruyère
🌐 www.domaine-labruyere.com	◉ Moulin-à-Vent [map p. 39]
🎫 🏭 🍇 🚜	14 ha; 58,000 btl

This is the original domain of the Labruyère family, which dates from 1870 when Jean-Marie Labruyère bought 10 ha in Romanèche-Thorins. Édouard Labruyère took over from his father Jean-Pierre in 2008. The Labruyères have expanded into other appellations, by buying Domaine Jacques Prieur in Meursault (in 1988), Château Rouget in Pomerol (1992), as well as starting Champagne Labruyère (2012). Nadine Gublin, the winemaker from Jacques Prieur, comes to the domain to make the wines. The domain makes single-parcel wines from three *climats* of Moulin-à-Vent: Le Clos is a 1 ha plot adjacent to the famous windmill with 70-year-old vines, Le Carquelin has 50-year-old vines on sandy clay, and Champ de Cour has 50-year-old vines on pebbly soil on granite. (The plots are similar to those of Château St. Jacques; see profile). Coeur de Terroir is an assemblage from various plots. Winemaking is Burgundian and starts with 3 days cold

81

maceration. The grapes for the single-parcel wines are completely destemmed (so fermentation is conventional, with no carbonic maceration) and then age for 16-20 months in demi-muids; Coeur de Terroir has been vinified as whole clusters since 2014, and then ages for 14 months in demi-muids. All the wines spend a further 3-6 months aging in concrete before bottling.

Domaine Lafarge-Vial

Chemin de Propières, 69820 Fleurie	📞 *+33 4 74 60 48 32*
@ *contact@lafargevial.com*	👤 *Frédéric Lafarge*
🚫 ◪ 🍇 ⚙ ◯ *6 ha; 20,000 btl*	◉ *Fleurie [map p. 39]*

In addition to running Domaine Lafarge in Volnay, Frédéric and Chantal Lafarge decided to start a new venture in 2014, starting by purchasing 2.25 ha in Beaujolais to explore another variety (Gamay) and new terroirs. The first vintage produced three cuvées: a Chiroubles, and two cuvées from Fleurie, Bel Air and Clos Vernay. Some more plots were purchased in time for the 2015 harvest, adding the Joie du Palais cuvée (from a slope so steep it has to be worked by horse). Vinification is Burgundian: complete destemming, conventional fermentation, aging in old barriques. "We want to make terroir wine, not Gamay," says Chantal.

Château de Lavernette

70, chemin de la Vernette, 71570 Leynes	📞 *+33 3 85 35 63 21*
@ *chateau@lavernette.com*	👤 *Xavier de Boissieu*
🌐 *www.lavernette.com*	◉ *Beaujolais Villages [map p. 38]*
🎫 🏭 🍇 ⚙ ◯	*14 ha; 60,000 btl*

The estate sits right at the junction between Mâcon and Beaujolais, with 11 ha to the west on granite at Leynes in Beaujolais AOP, and 3 ha to the east on clay-limestone at Chaintré in Pouilly Fuissé AOP. It originally belonged to the abbey of Tournus. The Lavernette family purchased the property in 1596, and it has stayed in the same family ever since. Bertrand and Anke de Boissieu took the estate out of the cooperative to start producing wine in 1988. Their son Xavier spent time in the United States, and returned in 2003 with his wife Kerrie, an oenologue. Xavier was the thirteenth generation when he took over in 2007 from his parents. There is a wide range of cuvées. There are both Beaujolais Blanc (from younger vines) and Bourgogne Blanc (from older vines). There are three cuvées from different holdings in Pouilly-Fuissé, and three from Beaujolais: Beaujolais Villages, Beaujolais-Leynes (Le Clos), and Beaujolais-Leynes Cuvée Jadis. Both the cuvées from Leynes finish fermentation in used barriques and then age in them for 10 and 22 months respectively. There's also a Crémant de Bourgogne (from the Chardonnay vineyard) and a sparkling wine from Gamay, called Granit.

Domaine Léonis

Les Presles, 69910 Villié-Morgon	📞 *+33 9 51 58 17 34*
	👤 *Raphael & Cristelle Champier*
🌐 *www.domaine-leonis.fr*	◉ *Morgon [map p. 41]*
🍇 🍇 🐌 ⊘	*8 ha; 25,000 btl*

82

Raphael Champier comes from a winemaking family, and spent six years working at Jean-Claude Lapalu before starting his own domain with Christine (formerly a photographer). They bought the first parcel of 0.5 he in Beaujolais Villages in 2011, and now have three plots in the Villages (two with 80-year-old vines), two plots in Brouilly (with 70-75-year old vines), a plot in Côte de Brouilly (the bottom half with 90-year old vines, the top half with even older vines). They restructured the vineyards in 2015 and moved into winery space in Villié-Morgon. They produce natural wines: manual harvesting, vinification of whole bunches, aging in barrels and vats, and bottling by the phase of the moon. They produce two cuvées from each appellation, one aged mostly or solely in concrete, and one aged partially or wholly in barriques. In Beaujolais Villages, Lurons is the entry-level, aged in concrete for 7 months, while Buissonnante ages partly in concrete and partly in barrels. There is also a Beaujolais Villages Blanc. From Brouilly, Brulius ages partly in concrete and partly in barrels, while Cuvée No. 1 ages in used barriques. From Côte de Brouilly, Mont Brulius ages in concrete, and Cuvée No. 2 ages in old barriques. Léonis is a Vin de France where the wine ferments and ages in a 500-liter amphora.

Thibault Liger-Belair

Lieu-dit Maison Neuve, 69840 Chénas	📞 *+33 3 80 61 51 16*
@ *contact@thibaultligerbelair.com*	👤 *Thibault Liger-Belair*
🌐 *www.thibaultligerbelair.com*	🗺 *Chénas [map p. 39]*
📋 ⚒ 🍇 🍂 ◯ 😊	*13 ha; 30,000 btl*

Coming from an old winemaking family that lost its vineyards, Thibault Liger-Belair established his domain at Nuits St. Georges in 2001. Having previously spent time in Beaujolais, he extended his activities by starting another domain in Moulin à Vent in 2009, initially with only 3.5 ha. The domain is called Pierres Roses, but the label says simply, Thibault Liger-Belair. His approach is Burgundian: "the object is to understand and produce wines representing their terroir and variety (Gamay)." He produces 6 cuvées from different plots, including a Vieilles Vignes and a Vignes Centenaires, and a Beaujolais Villages.

Domaine de la Madone Le Perréon

118 Boulevard Crozel-Mansard, 69460 Le Perréon	📞 *+33 6 80 33 42 42*
@ *bruno.bererd@orange.fr*	👤 *Bruno Bererd*
🌐 *www.facebook.com/profile.php?name=100063752491829*	🗺 *Beaujolais Villages [map p. 38]*
🚶 🏭 🍇 🚜	*29 ha*

The two Domaines de la Madone in Beaujolais should not be confused. One is in Fleurie, owned by the Despres family, taking its name from the chapel on the Madone hill. The other, formally with Le Perréon added to the name, is in the southern part of Beaujolais, with some of the highest vineyard plots in the area, over 500m altitude on very steep slopes. (Le Perréon is the name of the hill.) The estate dates from the 1940s and is now run by brothers Olivier and Bruno Bererd. Vines have an average age of 50 years; the oldest were planted in 1941. Beaujolais Nouveau is made from the bottom of the slope, and Beaujolais Villages from the upper plots, where the soil of pink granite is similar to

83

that of the Crus. Harvesting is manual. The wines are made by semi-carbonic maceration. There are two cuvées of Beaujolais Villages (labeled as Le Perréon with the name of the village). Tradition ages in concrete, and Fût de Chêne (made in small amounts) ages in oak including some new. 2 ha of white grapes are planted on slopes facing north.

Domaine Manoir du Carra

Le Carra, 69640 Denicé	📞 *+33 4 74 67 38 24*
@ *jfsambardier@manoir-du-carra.com*	👤 *Damien & Jean-Frédéric Sambardier*
🌐 *www.manoir-du-carra.com*	🔵 *Beaujolais Villages [map p. 38]*
🏠 🏭 🍇 🍷	*37 ha; 220,000 btl*

The vineyard dates from 1850. The estate was only 4 ha when Jean Sambardier, who had been working there, purchased it. His son Jean-Noël took over in 1972, and now works with his sons Jean-Frédéric and Damien. Vineyards have been considerably expanded to include plots in Beaujolais Villages, Brouilly, Fleurie, Juliénas, and Moulin à Vent. Vinification is by semi-carbonic maceration, with aging for about 4 months in old oak casks, except for Moulin à Vent, which ages in barriques.

Domaine des Marrans

109, route des Marrans, 69820 Fleurie	📞 *+33 4 74 04 13 21*
@ *contact@domainedesmarrans.com*	👤 *Mathieu & Camille Mélinand*
🌐 *www.domainedesmarrans.com*	🔵 *Fleurie [map p. 39]*
🏠 🏭 🍇 🍷	*20 ha; 100,000 btl*

Jean-Jacques Mélinand started making wine from 4 ha in Fleurie in 1970. He expanded the domain, mostly in Fleurie, and in 1989 needed to build a new winery, which he expanded in 2002. His son Mathieu joined the domain in 2009 after working in the New World, and added plots in Chiroubles and Morgon. Mathieu's arrival gave a new dynamic, to the point at which Jean-Jacques (known as JJ) introduces himself by saying, 'I am Mathieu's father'. Today the domain has 11 ha in Fleurie, 2.5 ha in Chiroubles, 2 ha in Morgon, and 3 ha in Beaujolais and Beaujolais Villages. Vinification is by semi-carbonic maceration. Beaujolais ages in tank; Beaujolais Villages ages in foudres for 8 months, and the Crus age in foudres for 12 months or more. The basic Fleurie is the largest cuvée, about a quarter of production, and there are also single-parcel cuvées from Fleurie. Holdings in the other crus are single parcels, so these are effectively single-vineyard wines also. All of the single-vineyard wines come from quite old vines. Fleurie Champagne comes from a 1.5 ha plot of 45-year old vines in the lieu-dit Champagne; Fleurie Latitude 46.17 comes from 45-year old vines in lieu-dit Les Marrans; Fleurie Clos du Pavillon comes from a 4 ha plot of 60-80-year old vines on pink granite. Morgon Corcelette comes from 45-year old vines; Chiroubles comes from 50-year old vines. Beaujolais Villages comes from old vines in Lancié; and there is also a Vieilles Vignes cuvée of Beaujolais.

Domaine Laurent Martray

Combiaty, 69460 Odenas	📞 *+33 6 14 42 04 74*
@ *martray.laurent@akeonet.com*	👤 *Laurent Martray*

🌐 www.domainelaurentmartray.com   🍇 Brouilly [map p. 41]

📅 🏭 🍇 🚜   5 ha; 30,000 btl

Laurence Martray's winery is located on the next hill over from the Château de la Chaize, from whom he rented half his vineyards until the lease expired. The domain contracted by about half when the lease with Château de la Chaize ran out, but the lost vineyards have been partially replaced by 2 ha at Pierreux near Château Thivin. Laurent has been making wine here from his estate and leased vineyards since 1987. The domain is mostly in Brouilly, where the soils are sand and silt on a base of granite. There's also a hectare on Côte de Brouilly, where soils are blue volcanic rocks of porphyry and diorite. The use of carbonic maceration is attenuated by destemming some of the grapes. The cuvées from Brouilly have different aging protocols: Vieilles Vignes ages in foudres and demi-muids, while Corentin (actually from vines older than the Vieilles Vignes) and La Folie (a cuvée added in 2016) age in barriques, as does the Côte de Brouilly.

Domaine Métrat et Fils

La Roilette, 69820 Fleurie	📞 +33 0 33 68 73 26
@ contact@domainemetrat.fr	👤 Bernard Métrat
🌐 www.domainemetrat.fr	🍇 Fleurie [map p. 39]
📅 🏭 🍇 🌿	10 ha; 40,000 btl

Located at La Roilette, on the slope leading from Fleurie to Moulin à Vent, this old family domain is now run by Bernard Métrat. From Fleurie there are two cuvées: La Roilette Tradition, and La Roilette Vieilles Vignes, from vines more than 60-years old. The Moulin à Vent also comes from old vines. The Chiroubles comes from a lieu-dit called Côte Rôtie, but the authorities banned the use of the name on the label because people might get confused with wines from Côte Rôtie in the Rhône! So Bernard relabeled it as La Scandaleuse. Winemaking is traditional, with fermentation by semi-carbonic maceration followed by aging in cement, but a small part of the Vieilles Vignes La Roilette and the Moulin à Vent are aged in old barriques.

Domaine des Montillets

Les Montillets, 69910 Villié Morgon	📞 +33 6 83 56 69 96
@ aurelien-large@orange.fr	👤 Marylène & Aurélien Large
🌐 www.domainedesmontillets.fr	🍇 Morgon [map p. 41]
📅 🏭 🍇 🌿	12 ha; 10,000 btl

This family domain has been handed from father to son for four generations. Marylène and Aurélien Large took over in 1999. The domain is located in the area of Les Montillets, just to the west of the Côte de Py; there are also plots at Javernières, just to the east of Côte de Py. Les Montillets is an assemblage from plots in Les Montillets (sandy over gravel) and Javernières (pebbly). Morgon Grand Âge comes from four plots of old vines in Les Montillets, planted between 1940 and 1958. Production is only 500 bottles. (It was previously called Montillets Tête de Cuvée.) The Javernières Première Arpent comes from vines planted in 1952 at Javernières. Vinification is by semi-carbonic maceration, followed by aging in stainless steel.

85

Maison Le Nid

Hameau Moulin À Vent, 71570 Romanèche-Thorins	📞 *+33 6 89 96 45 19*
@ *contact@lenid.fr*	👤 *Stéphane Lardet*
🌐 *www.lenid.fr*	🔴 *Moulin-à-Vent [map p. 39]*
🗓 🏭 🍇 🍷	*7 ha; 15,000 btl*

This was called the Domaine du Petit Chêne until it was purchased and renamed in 2012 by industrialist Paul Lardet, who works with his three children. Vineyards are divided into 12 parcels, all in Moulin à Vent. Cuvée Tradition is a blend from parcels over 4 ha, and La Rochelle and Rochegrès come from plots of under 1 ha in specific *climats*. After fermentation in stainless steel, the general blend, Tradition, ages in old foudres for 10 months; the elegance and structure of Moulin a Vent come through with a very fine impression on the palate. La Rochelle comes from 80-year-old vines in a plot between Rochegrès and Fleurie, and ages in used barriques for 15 months. Making quite a Burgundian impression, it has greater depth than Tradition; the main difference is the extra sense of refinement. Rochegrès ages in barriques from new to 3-year for 15 months and conveys a sense of richness and generosity above Tradition and La Rochelle.

Domaine des Nugues

40 rue de la Serve,69220 Lancié	📞 *+33 4 74 04 14 00*
@ *gilles@domainedesnugues.fr*	👤 *Gilles Gelin*
🌐 *www.domainedesnugues.com*	🔴 *Beaujolais Villages [map p. 39]*
🗓 🏭 🍇 🍷	*36 ha; 260,000 btl*

Gérard Gelin purchased the Clos des Nugues in 1976, and this became the heart of the Domaine. Gilles Gelin joined his father in 2000, and took over after Gérard retired in 2008. The domain has been steadily expanding; today most of its holdings are in Beaujolais and Beaujolais Villages, but there are 6 ha in Fleurie, 2 ha in Moulin à Vent, and 1 ha in Morgon, as well as a little Syrah, which goes into Elle & Lui, a Vin de France with 76% Syrah and 24% Gamay. There is also a sparkling Gamay, Made by G. They also make a crème de cassis. For Beaujolais, winemaking is traditional: fermentation by semi-carbonic maceration, followed by aging in cuve, except for the Morgon where one third ages in old barriques.

Christophe Pacalet

1910 Route des Crus, 69220 Cercié-en-Beaujolais	📞 *+33 4 74 04 43 94*
@ *contact@christophepacalet.com*	👤 *Christophe Pacalet*
🌐 *www.christophepacalet.com*	🔴 *Brouilly [map p. 41]*
🗓 🏭 🍇 🛢 🍷 🍇	*7 ha*

Christophe Pacalet started as a chef, then got his experience in winemaking by working with his uncle, Marcel Lapierre. He set up as a winemaker in 1999, not by buying vineyards but by purchasing grapes. (His cousin Philippe Pacalet takes a similar approach in Burgundy.) Technically Christophe is a negociant, but he doesn't deal in wine: in fact, he has his own team for harvesting the grapes he buys. Many of his sources come from the same plots each year; he focuses on plots with older vines and makes wine from about 8

86

ha. The range includes Beaujolais Nouveau, Beaujolais Villages, Beaujolais Blanc, and most of the Crus. Fermentation is by semi-carbonic maceration, and the Crus then age in a mix of foudres and old barriques. Christophe extended his activities in 2018 by buying the winery and 4 ha of vineyards of the Château des Labourons in Fleurie

Domaine Gilles Paris

44 rue des Sarments 69820 Fleurie	📞 *+33 4 74 69 12 48*
@ *gilles.earlparis@orange.fr*	👤 *Gilles Paris*
🗓 🏭 🌿 🚜 ⊘ *8 ha*	🔘 *Fleurie [map p. 39]*

Gilles Paris comes from a winegrowing family in Quincié-en-Beaujolais—his brothers are all involved with making wine—and he moved to Chiroubles, where his wife's family grew grapes for the coop. In 2005 he started making wine in Chiroubles under the label of C G Paris (Christine and Gilles Paris). After a divorce, there was period before Gilles was able to set up again, and he moved to a new winery in Fleurie in 2017. Wines are labeled as Domaine Gilles Paris. He also distributes the wines for his brother Jérôme, whose label is very similar to the C G Paris label. He has 4.5 ha in Chiroubles and smaller plots in Morgon and Fleurie. In 2016 his vineyards were almost destroyed by hail, and he made wine from purchased grapes. The Chiroubles Cuvée Terroir is the flagship of the domain; Morgon Douby comes from 50-year-old vines; Fleurie Grand Pré comes from three parcels in the lieu-dit, and there is also Fleurie Champagne from another lieu-dit.

Domaine Passot Collonge

210, impasse du Colombier,, 69910 Villié Morgon	📞 *+33 4 74 69 10 77*
@ *mbpassot@yahoo.fr*	👤 *Bernard & Monique Passot*
⊕ *www.passotcollonge.fr*	🔘 *Morgon [map p. 41]*
🗓 🏭 📦 🌿 🌯	*6 ha; 15,000 btl*

Bernard and Monique Passot established the domain in 1990 with vines coming from both sides of the family, the Passots from Chiroubles and Fleurie, and the Collanges from Villié-Morgon. Their son Jean-Guillaume joined in 2005. Grapes from most of the Crus are destemmed for a short conventional fermentation, followed by a few months aging in concrete. The Morgon Vieilles Vignes ages in oak. Cuvées from specific *climats* in Morgon are Les Charmes, Douby, and Côte de Py.

Domaine Laurent Perrachon et fils

Domaine des Mouilles, 69840 Juliénas	📞 *+33 4 74 04 40 44*
@ *domaine@vinsperrachon.com*	👤 *Maxime & Adrien Perrachon*
⊕ *www.vinsperrachon.com*	🔘 *Juliénas [map p. 39]*
🗓 🏭 🌿 🚜	*30 ha; 120,000 btl*

The Perrachon family settled in Juliénas in 1601, and the domain dates from 1877, when the family bough the La Bottière estate in Juliénas. Several generations later, in the hands of cousins Laurent and Pierre-Yves, it has acquired an unusually wide range of Crus in Beaujolais. Domaine des Mouilles in Juliénas is now the core of the domain, they have

87

owned Domaine des Perelles in Moulin-à-Vent for a long time, and more recently have added smaller plots in Morgon, Fleurie, Chénas, and Saint-Amour. As well as a range of generic AOP wines, Beaujolais Villages and Nouveau, Blanc and rosé, there are generic cuvées from each Cru, plus single-parcel wines from Juliénas, Morgon, and Moulin-à-Vent. From Juliénas there are two communal cuvées: Roche Bleue from the original estate at La Bottières, and Les Mouilles. The special cuvées from Juliénas are Vignes Centenaires, from a one hectare plot of 100-year-old vines at La Bottière; and l'Irréstible from a selection of the best plots. More than a quarter of production comes from Juliénas. In Morgon the top cuvée comes from a half-hectare parcel on Côte du Py. All the wines start by semi-carbonic maceration. The top cuvées, have extended aging of 12 months in barriques followed by three months in large oak vats. The special cuvée from Moulin-à-Vent, Les Burdelines, ages in new oak.

Robert Perroud

Les Balloquets, 69460 Odenas	📞 +33 4 74 04 35 63
@ robertperroud@wanadoo.fr	👤 Robert Perroud
🌐 www.robert-perroud.com	Brouilly [map p. 41]
🗓 ⛰ 🍇 🚜	13 ha; 60,000 btl

The estate has been owned by the Perroud family since the French Revolution in 1789. Robert is the seventh generation. His range of ten wines includes three from Brouilly, two from Côte de Brouilly, Beaujolais Blanc, and red and white Bourgogne, and a Viognier Vin de France. The winery is located near the lieu-dit of Les Balloquets, with a very steep slope (40%). The l'Enfer de Balloquets cuvée of Brouilly comes from the slope, the Pollen cuvée is a step up, and Cuvée Romain comes from a single plot facing east.

Domaine des Pierres

2220 Route de Juliénas, 71570 La Chapelle de Guinchay	📞 +33 6 88 74 55 78
@ trichardjf@orange.fr	👤 Jean-François Trichard
🌐 www.domaine-des-pierres.fr	Moulin-à-Vent [map p. 39]
🗓 ⛰ 🍇 🚜	20 ha; 55,000 btl

Jean-François Trichard has accumulated a series of holdings in Beaujolais and Mâcon from his family. He started with the Domaine des Pierres in Moulin à Vent, which he uncle Georges Trichard had founded in 1964, and passed to him in 2005. In 2011 he obtained part of the Domaine du Roy de Croix in Mâcon-Chaintré and Pouilly Fuissé from his in-laws, and then in 2017 his father retired, bringing him vineyards in Moulin à Vent and Juliénas. All the wines are labeled Domaine des Pierres quite discreetly, with Jean-François Trichard appearing in somewhat larger letters. Vinification is by carbonic maceration; the top cuvées age in oak.

Château de Pierreux

Pierreux, 69460 Odenas	📞 +33 4 74 03 42 16
@ contact@chateaudepierreux.com	
🌐 www.chateaudepierreux.com	Brouilly [map p. 41]
🌙 🖊 🍇 🌱	110 ha

88

Château de Pierreux is rather a grand estate for the Beaujolais, dating from a fortified manor house of the 13th century, with cellars from the 17th century, and most of the building constructed in the 19th century. Located at the foot of Mont Brouilly, it has been part of Jean-Claude Boisset's portfolio since 2002. The extensive vineyards are on the sandy soil on top of pink granite characteristic of the area. Vines have been mostly converted from growing as individual bushes to training on a relatively high cordon in rows. Grapes are destemmed (so fermentation is conventional, not by semi-carbonic maceration). The range starts with the Réserve du Château, which ages in large wood vats for 6 months. Lieu-dit Pierreux comes from two plots, and ages for 6 month in oak. Terre de Pierreux was introduced in 2017 as cuvée from two plots, one the classic sand over pink granite, the other with much more clay, together only a little over 1 ha, with vines that are 40- or 60-years-old, still growing as individual bushes. It ages for 24 months in oak. The Grande Réserve comes from 85-year old bush vines, is made only in the best years, and ages for 6 months in oak.

Roland Pignard

Saint-Joseph, 69910 Villié Morgon	📞 *+33 4 74 69 90 73*
@ *r.j.pignard@wanadoo.fr*	👤 *Roland & Joëlle Pignard*
🌐 *www.rolandpignard.fr*	⚙ *Morgon [map p. 41]*
🚶 🏭 🍇 🚜 🗂	*5 ha*

Roland Pignard took over his 10 ha family estate in 1977. He began trials with organic viticulture in the late 1980s, and by 2004 decided to change his approach. He reduced the size of the estate to 4.5 ha, with plots in Beaujolais Villages, Regnié, and Morgon. Whole bunches are fermented with maceration lasting 4 days for Beaujolais Villages, 6 days for Regnié, and 9 days for Morgon. The vines are all old, 40 years for Beaujolais Villages, 50 years for Regnié, and 60 years for Morgon. Wines age in concrete, except for Morgon Tradition, which ages for 12 months in barriques.

Domaine Des Pins

120 rue de la Piat, 71570 Saint Amour Bellevue	📞 *+33 6 61 77 32 94*
@ *joseph.de-sonis@orange.fr*	👤 *Joseph de Sonis*
🌐 *www.domainedespins.fr*	⚙ *Saint Amour [map p. 39]*
🔲 🏭 🍇 🍃 ⊘	*9 ha; 65,000 btl*

The name comes from the century-old pine trees are around the property (although many were destroyed in a storm in 1999). The soils of the surrounding vineyards vary from sandstone to marl and sand. Most of the plantings are Gamay, but there is some Chardonnay for a Beaujolais Villages Blanc. Joseph de Sonis bought the property in 2016, and renovated the cellars and replanted some plots in 2017. The range of reds starts with Gourmandise des Pins and Tradition des Pins. The top red is Prestige des Pins, which seems some aging in oak; there is also a cuvée with no added sulfur, La Folie.

Domaine de la Pirolette

La Pirolette, 71570 Saint Amour Bellevue	📞 *+33 6 75 06 22 73*

89

@ *domainedelapirolette@gmail.com*	🧍 *Gregory Barbet*
⊕ *domainedelapirolette.com*	◉ *Saint Amour [map p. 39]*
🗓️ 🏔️ 🍇 🚜	*15 ha*

This domain took its current form almost by accident. Newly married, Gregory and Virginie Barbet were looking for a house in Beaujolais, and Gregory's father, Xavier, of the Domaine des Billards (see profile), suggested they should buy a property in Saint Amour which came with vineyards. Just on top of the hill, the domain overlooks the village, which has become known for its two Michelin-starred restaurants. The first harvest was in 2013. The 12 parcels are all in Saint Amour, on soils varying from pink granite to blue granite and to flinty clay. Wine are fermented in cement using the châpeau grillé method, in which a wooden grate keeps the skins submerged, and the juice is regularly pumped over. Aging is in stainless steel, although cement eggs are used for some single-vineyard wines (first release in 2019).

Château de Poncié

1087 Route de Poncié, 69820 Fleurie	📞 *+33 4 74 69 83 33*
@ *contact@chateaudeponcie.fr*	🧍 *Marion Fessy*
⊕ *www.chateaudeponcie.fr*	◉ *Fleurie [map p. 39]*
🚶 🏔️ 🍇 🍇	*40 ha; 96,000 btl*

Known by its Latin name, Villa Ponciago, the estate was given to the Abbey of Cluny in 949. An eighteenth century map shows the château surrounded by vineyards. Today's estate covers 120 ha, with under half planted to vines in 40 different parcels; the rest of the estate has fields and woods. The name changed to Château de Poncié, until the Henriot family, who own Bouchard Père et Fils in Beaune and William Fèvre in Chablis, bought the estate in 2008. It was then sold in 2020 to an entrepreneur from Lyon, Jean-Loup Rogé. Marion Fessy came as director (she had been the director of her family estate, Henry Fessy). Production here is Burgundian (no carbonic maceration), starting with cold maceration, partial destemming, conventional fermentation in small vats, and aging in barriques as well as cuve. Fleurie Le Pré Roi is a blend from four parcels, aged 20-30% in barriques of 1-4-years, La Salomine ages 40-60% in barriques, and Les Moriers ages entirely in barriques. There is also a Beaujolais Villages Blanc, Grande Lamure, from 2 ha of Chardonnay, aged in 3-4-year barriques. Under Henriot, Villa Ponciago was used to describe a wider range of wines that included purchased grapes, including Beaujolais Villages and several cuvées from Fleurie, Moulin-à-Vent, and Brouilly.

Château de Raousset

21 route de Verchère, Chiroubles	📞 *+33 4 74 69 17 28*
@ *info@chateauderaousset.com*	🧍 *Claire Reber*
⊕ *www.chateauderaousset.com*	◉ *Chiroubles [map p. 39]*
🚶 🏔️ 🍇 ☘️	*25 ha; 60,000 btl*

The domain owes its name to its founder in the nineteenth century. It took its present form, with parcels in Chiroubles, the Douby *climat* in Morgon, and Grille Midi in Fleurie, under Gaston de Raousset, who ran it for the first half of the twentieth century. The

90

Chiroubles Bel Air is vinified by semi-carbonic maceration and aged in concrete. Fleurie Grille Midi comes from 50-year-old vines and is vinified similarly; cuvée Gaston de Raousset from Fleurie ages in old oak foudres. The two cuvées from Morgon age in old oak casks. A small production of Beaujolais Villages Blanc ages in stainless steel.

Château des Ravatys

37 route de Ravatys, 69220 Saint-Lager	📞 *+33 4 74 66 80 35*
@ *contact@chateaudesravatys.com*	👤 *Aurélie De Vermont*
🌐 *www.chateaudesravatys.com*	🔴 *Beaujolais Villages [map p. 41]*
🚶 🏭 🍇 🚜	*29 ha; 150,000 btl*

The Château des Ravatys has an unusual history. An old winemaking domaine, it was bought in the nineteenth century by Auguste Solet, an engineer who had made a fortune in Algeria. His niece Mathilde Courbe inherited the property in 1879, and in 1937 she left her estate to the Institut Pasteur. The vineyards were expanded by a gift from another source in Côte de Brouilly, in 2002. They comprise 20 ha in Côte de Brouilly and 8 ha in Brouilly. The Pasteur Institut not only made wine here, but after renovations in 1990 developed the château as a center for meetings and other events. Profits all go to supporting the Institut. Wines are from Brouilly and Côte de Brouilly. The Brouilly ages in cuve, while Brouilly le Marquisat ages in foudres. Côte de Brouilly and the Cuvée Louis Pasteur age half in foudre and half in barriques, Mathilde Courbe in foudre, and Réserve de Ravatys in barriques. The Institut sold the property in 2021 to raise funds to support research, and it was purchased by the Lavorel hotel and restaurant group.

Domaine Richard Rottiers

Sambinerie, 71570 Romanèche-Thorins	📞 *+33 3 85 35 22 36*
@ *contact@domainerichardrottiers.com*	👤 *Richard Rottiers*
🌐 *www.domainerichardrottiers.com*	🔴 *Moulin-à-Vent [map p. 39]*
📅 🏭 🍇 🛢 🍇	*10 ha; 60,000 btl*

Richard Rottiers comes from Chablis, and gained experience in a variety of vineyards in the New World as well as France before buying 3 ha of old vineyards in Moulin à Vent in 2007. He produces three cuvées of Moulin à Vent: the village wine goes through semi-carbonic maceration and then ages for 6 months in a mix of foudres and barriques; Dernier Souffle come from a 60-year-old plot and ages for 8 months in barriques; and *Climat* Champ de Cour ages for 10 months in barriques. The Beaujolais Villages ages in foudres and barriques. There's also a sparkling rosé. In 2018 he took over the family Domaine des Malandes in Chablis together with his sister, and now makes wine there as well as in Beaujolais.

Domaine Roches Bleues

route Mont Brouilly, 69460 Odenas	📞 *+33 6 17 38 11 71*
@ *contact@domainelesrochesbleues.com*	👤 *Jonathan Buisson*
🌐 *www.domainelesrochesbleues.com*	🔴 *Brouilly [map p. 41]*
🚶 🏭 🍇 🍇	*9 ha*

91

Located on the slopes south of Mont Brouilly, this family domain is now in its third generation. Annie and Louis Bassy acquired the first 4 ha in 1967. The next generation, Christiane and Dominique Lacondemine, took over in 1993, and Jonathan and Chloé Buisson took over in 2019. Vineyards are in both Brouilly and Côte de Brouilly, with an average age of 50 years. Wines are fermented by semi-carbonic maceration. The range starts with Brouilly La Croquant, aged in concrete. The rest of the range ages in foudres. Brouilly Les 3 Loups comes from a parcel on blue rocks, and Les Mignonnes de Pierreux comes from several parcels on volcanic rocks and schist. From Côte de Brouilly, Soleil de Brulhié comes from the climat Brulhié on granitic and volcanic terroir, De Lys comes from the oldest (60-80year) vines in Brulhié, and L'Héronde comes from a parcel on volcanic blue rocks.

Domaine Rochette

460 route du Chalet, 69430 Régnié-Durette	📞 +33 6 68 08 84 91
@ vinsdomainerochette@orange.fr	👤 Matthieu & Chantal Rochette
🌐 vinsdomainerochette.fr	🔴 Régnié [map p. 41]
🛑 🏭 🍇 🍃	12 ha; 45,000 btl

Located at 300m altitude on the slopes of the Vallée de l'Ardières, southwest of Villié-Morgon, this family domain passed from Joël Rochette (who established the domain in 1981) to his son Matthieu and Matthieu's wife Chantal, in 2009. There's a range of Beaujolais and Beaujolais Villages in all three colors, and cuvées from four Crus. Wines ferment by semi-carbonic maceration in stainless steel. Regnié is the largest production (just under half of all production), and there's also a Regnié Cuvée des Braves, from a parcel of 50-year old vines. There are single cuvées from Brouilly and Côte de Brouilly, and four cuvées from two *climats* in Morgon: Les Micouds, Côte du Puy and a separate cuvée from Côte du Puy, Fût de Chêne, which sees oak aging, and Cuvée XVII from Côte du Puy, aged in a demi-muid.

Domaine Romanesca

1172 Route de la Chapelle des Bois. 69820 Fleurie	📞 +33 6 82 19 90 80
@ contact.domaineromanesca@gmail.com	👤 Olivier Chastel
🌐 www.domaineromanesca.com	🔴 Fleurie [map p. 39]
🚶 🏭 🍇 🍃	12 ha; 15,000 btl

Guy and Ferréole Chastel developed this small domain, with more than half of its holdings in two *climats* of Moulin à Vent. Their sons, twins Antoine and Olivier, now run the estate, and have added plots in Fleurie, Juliénas, and Morgon. Each Moulin à Vent *climat* makes an individual cuvée. They ferment by semi-carbonic maceration, and then Champ de Cour ages for a year in concrete, while La Rochelle ages for a year in oak. Fleurie La Chapelle des Bois ages in concrete, while Juliénas Les Fouillouses ages in 5-year barriques. There are also Beaujolais Villages Blanc, rosé, and pétillant.

Domaine Ruet

178 route du Château, 69220 Cercié-en-Beaujolais	📞 +33 4 74 66 85 00
@ contact@ruet-beaujolais.fr	👤 Katy & David Duthel

92

⊕ *ruet-beaujolais.fr*	◉ *Brouilly [map p. 41]*
🗓 ⛏ 🍇 🥄	*20 ha; 120,000 btl*

The domain was established in 1926 by Katy Duthel's great grandfather. David Duthel worked at the domain, then left in 2003 to run his own domain, Père Dudu in Morgon, and then returned five years later to take over Domaine Ruet with Katy. This added three cuvées of Morgon to the range. Vinification uses semi-carbonic maceration, but there can be adjustments to destem some grapes depending on the year. Regnié, Brouilly, Chiroubles, Morgon Douby, and Morgon Grands Cras, all age in concrete or stainless steel, Côte de Brouilly ages in a mix of vats and foudres, and Morgon Côte du Py ages in foudres. There are also Beaujolais, Beaujolais Villages, Bourgogne Rouge and Blanc, and a Pinot Noir from IGP Comtés-Rhodaniens.

Domaine Saint-Cyr

Les Perrelles, 69480 Anse	📞 *+33 4 74 60 23 69*
@ *email@beaujolais-saintcyr.com*	👤 *Raphaël Saint Cyr*
⊕ *www.beaujolais-saintcyr.com*	◉ *Beaujolais [map p. 38]*
🧍 ⛏ 🍇 ✿	*27 ha; 100,000 btl*

Raphaël Saint-Cyr's grandfather created the estate by renting 13 ha in 1963 in the south of Beaujolais in the Pierre Dorées area under the name of Domaine de Bellevue. The wine was sold to negociants until the next generation started estate-bottling in 1983. New cellars were built in 1999. Raphaël took over in 2008. In addition to the 20 ha in Beaujolais AOP, wine is now made from several crus: Chénas (3 ha), Moulin à Vent (1.5 ha), Morgon (1 ha), and Regnié (1 ha). Each of the crus is a single plot, and the name of the lieu-dit is shown on the label. All harvesting is manual. The largest production is the estate Beaujolais, Les Pierres Dorées, which after fermentation in concrete, ages for 9 months in cuve but with one third spending 6 months in barriques to add some structure. There is also the cuvée Terroir de Bellevue, described as "vinified naturally to express the terroir," which has longer maceration and fermentation and ages only in cuve. The Crus are vinified following more Burgundian lines, with complete destemming, long maceration and fermentation, and aging for 18 months, two thirds in cuve and one third in barriques.

Anthony Thévenet

92 impasse de l'Ouby, 69910 Villié Morgon	📞 *+33 6 61 62 92 45*
@ *anthony.thevenet@bbox.fr*	👤 *Anthony Thévenet*
🗓 ⛏ 🍇 🥄 🏆 *7 ha; 45,000 btl*	◉ *Morgon [map p. 41]*

Anthony Thévenet had an apprenticeship with Georges Descombes (see profile) and then was working at Jean Foillard when he inherited 3 ha of vines from his grandfather in 2010. He started to make his own wine in 2013, while continuing to work at Foillard. He inherited a parcel in Morgon Côte de Py in 2014, and added some further plots in Beaujolais Villages and Chénas in 2017, when he took on the domain full-time. The top cuvées are Julia, from 80-year old vines on the Côte de Py, and the Morgon Vieilles Vignes, from two plots of old vines, one pre-phylloxera 150-year old vines, the other 80-year old.

93

Fermentation is semi-carbonic, then the wines age in concrete, except for the top two Morgons, which age in old wood.

Charly Thévenet

Lieu Dit Le Clachet, 69910 Villié Morgon	📞 *+33 4 74 66 39 93*
@ *charly-thevenet@hotmail.fr*	👤 *Charly Thévenet*
🔲 🏭 🐝 🚜 🔵 ⓒ 🍇 *3 ha; 10,000 btl*	🌍 *Morgon [map p. 41]*

Charly is the son of Jean-Paul Thévenet (see profile), one of the Gang of Four who reintroduced artisanal winemaking to Beaujolais in the 1980s. After working with Jean-Paul and with Marcel Lapierre, in 2007 Charly purchased some 80-year-old vines in Regnié. The site has two plots, one south-facing, the other southwest. Charly ferments them separately, and then blends for bottling into his single cuvée, Grain et Granit. He harvests late to get good ripeness, ferments by semi-carbonic maceration, and ages in old barriques. The style is elegant and Burgundian. The cuvée Tradition from Morgon shows the stern side of the Cru on top of Charly's elegant style, and usually needs an extra year before it is ready. Production is tiny, but Charly is regarded as a rising star in Beaujolais.

Jean-Paul Thévenet

Le Clachet, 69910 Villié Morgon	📞 *+33 4 74 66 39 93*
@ *jeanpaulthevenet@yahoo.fr*	👤 *Jean-Paul Thévenet*
🐝 🚜 ⓒ 🍇 *5 ha; 24,000 btl*	🌍 *Morgon [map p. 41]*

The Thévenets have had vineyards in Morgon since 1870. One of the Gang of Four (together with Lapierre, Foillard, and Breton) who reintroduced artisanal winemaking in Beaujolais in the 1980s, Jean-Paul has two plots in Morgon of 45-year and 110-year old vines. He harvests late, ferments by semi-carbonic maceration in cement, and ages the wine in old barriques. There are two cuvées from Morgon: Cuvée Tradition Le Clachet (named for the lieu-dit) and the Vieilles Vignes, from the oldest vines. He also makes a light sparkling Gamay, On Pète La Soif. He is helped by his son, who also makes his own wine from Regnié under the label Charly Thévenet (see profile).

Domaine Thillardon

Les Brureaux, 69840 Chénas	📞 *+33 6 07 76 00 91*
@ *paul-henri.t@hotmail.fr*	👤 *Paul-Henri & Charles Thillardon*
🌐 *domainethillardon.com*	🌍 *Chénas [map p. 39]*
🔲 🏭 🐝 🚜 ⓒ 🍇	*12 ha; 40,000 btl*

Paul-Henri Thillardon started out by renting vineyards in Chénas in 2008 when he was only 22. By 2012 he was able to purchase the vineyards of the Domaine des Chassignols with very old vines next to Moulin à Vent, and in 2014 his brother joined him. The domain now has 4 ha in Chénas and 3 ha in Moulin à Vent as well as various other small plots. Winemaking has a mix of influences: grapes are mostly destemmed, and aging is in a mix of cement and old wood. The Thillardon brothers have a Burgundian interest in terroir, and there are often micro-cuvées made from specific plots.

94

Château Thivin

630, route du Mont Brouilly, 69460 Odenas	📞 +33 4 74 03 47 53
@ geoffray@chateau-thivin.com	👤 Claude Geoffray
🌐 www.chateau-thivin.com	🔴 Brouilly [map p. 41]
🗓 🍇 🍇 🍂	27 ha; 140,000 btl

Wine has been made here for centuries—the château itself was built in the fourteenth century—but the modern era started when Zaccharie Geoffray purchased the château in 1877 with a couple of hectares. Two generations later, Claude Geoffray was involved in the creation of the Côte de Brouilly AOC. The domain was created in 1953. Still in the hands of the same family, it is now run by (another) Claude Geoffray and his son Claude-Édouard. In addition to Beaujolais and Beaujolais Villages, there are Brouilly and several cuvées of Côte de Brouilly. All undergo semi-carbonic maceration. The Crus are aged in old foudres. The Côte de Brouilly is a blend from seven plots, La Chapelle comes from a 2 ha parcel at the top of the slope, and Zaccharie is a blend from several parcels that is aged in barriques, with 5-10% new oak.

Domaine de Thulon

2 chemin de Thulon, 69430 Lantignié	📞 +33 4 74 04 80 29
@ carine@thulon.com	👤 Carine & Laurent Jambon
🌐 thulon.com	🔴 Régnié [map p. 41]
🗓 🍇 🍇 ☍	18 ha; 90,000 btl

René and Annie Jambon worked the vineyards of the Domaine de Thulon for twenty years before they bought the property, which was then only 8 ha. Their son Laurent now makes the wine, and his sister Carine runs the commercial side. Grapes are partly de-stemmed, and fermentation is followed by aging in cuve. The range starts with Beaujolais Villages in all three colors, including a special cuvée of the Villages rouge, La Cerise Sur le Gâteau, and there are two unusual cuvées of Viognier, one dry and one sweet. From the Crus there are Régnié, Chiroubles, and Morgon Charmes. There are two cuvées of Beaujolais Villages, both from Lantignié, for which the grapes are completely de-stemmed: 1947-1er ages for 12 months in barriques and 6 months in cuve; Opale ages in barrels of various sizes.

Château des Tours

69460 Saint Étienne la Varenne	📞 +33 4 74 03 40 86
@ chateaudestours@wanadoo.fr	👤 Vins Richard
🌐 www.chateau-des-tours.com	🔴 Brouilly [map p. 41]
🗓 🍇 🏠 🍇 🚜	70 ha

With its holdings including a single block of 48 ha at the base of Mont Brouilly, this is an emblematic domain for the appellation. The history dates from the fourteenth century—the château originated as a fortress—and the estate was bought by its present owners, Vins Richard, in 1986. They also own Château de Corcelles, also in Brouilly, Château La Nerthe in Châteauneuf-du-Pape, and other properties in the Southern Rhône and Bordeaux. Château des Tours produces both Brouilly (from vines with an average age of 45 years) and a Vieilles Vignes cuvée (from 60-year-old vines). Vinification is conventional, and the Brouilly ages in cuve, while the Vieilles Vignes ages in oak. The style tends to freshness.

Domaine de la Voûte des Crozes

Les Crozes, 80 Grand Rue, 69220 Cercié-en-Beaujolais	📞 *+33 4 74 66 80 37*
@ *chanrion.nicole@wanadoo.fr*	👤 *Nicole & Romain Chanrion*
⊕ *www.vignoble-chanrion.com*	*Côte de Brouilly [map p. 41]*
🗒 🏭 🐛 😊	*6 ha; 30,000 btl*

This is a really hands-on family domain, now in its sixth generation. Since Nicole Chanrion took over from her father in 1988, she has worked the vineyards and made the wine more or less single-handed until she was joined by her son, Romain. She became President of the Côte de Brouilly growers' association in 2000. Vineyards are on volcanic blue schist. Fermentation is by semi-carbonic maceration, and then the wine ages in foudres for 9 months. In addition to the Côte de Brouilly (the main production), Perle de Gamay is a white wine made from a tiny plot of Gamay on clay soils, labeled as Vin de France, and Effervescence is a sparkling wine.

Jura

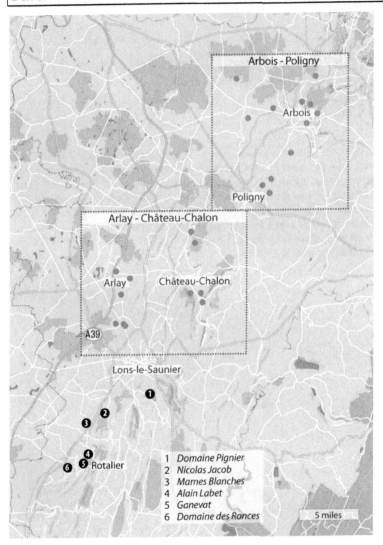

97

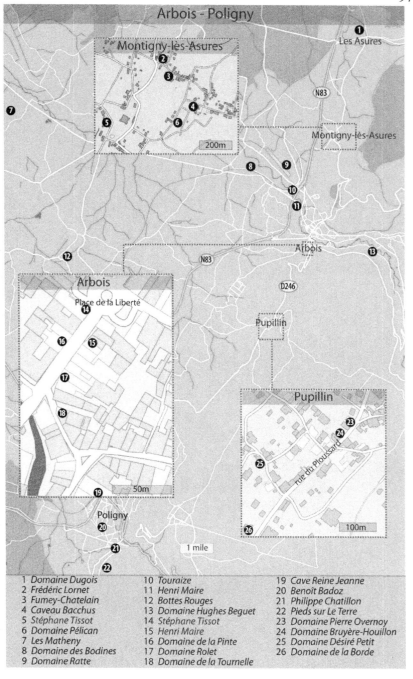

1 Domaine Dugois
2 Frédéric Lornet
3 Fumey-Chatelain
4 Caveau Bacchus
5 Stéphane Tissot
6 Domaine Pélican
7 Les Matheny
8 Domaine des Bodines
9 Domaine Ratte
10 Touraize
11 Henri Maire
12 Bottes Rouges
13 Domaine Hughes Beguet
14 Stéphane Tissot
15 Henri Maire
16 Domaine de la Pinte
17 Domaine Rolet
18 Domaine de la Tournelle
19 Cave Reine Jeanne
20 Benoît Badoz
21 Philippe Chatillon
22 Pieds sur Le Terre
23 Domaine Pierre Overnoy
24 Domaine Bruyère-Houillon
25 Domaine Désiré Petit
26 Domaine de la Borde

98

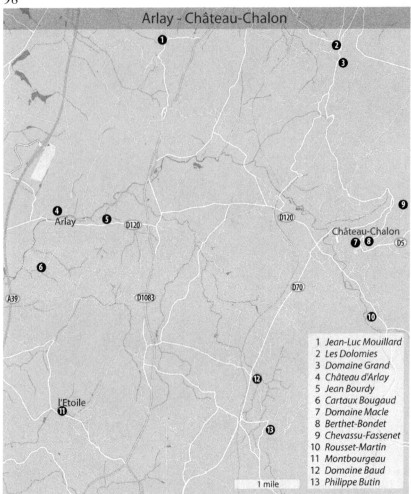

Profiles of Leading Estates

Domaine Berthet-Bondet *

7 rue de La Tour, 39210 Château-Chalon	☏ +33 3 84 44 60 48
@ domaine@berthet-bondet.com	👤 Hélène Berthet-Bondet
🌐 www.berthet-bondet.com	◎ Château-Chalon [map p. 98]
🔸 🏭 🍷 🍾 14 ha; 50,000 btl	🍾 Château-Chalon

Jean Berthet-Bondet started the domain in 1985; his family was not previously in wine. "I was attracted by wines and agronomie, I started, I worked abroad, my family had always liked Château-Chalon. The price of vineyards was attractive. People were pulling out vineyards; it was possible to buy." The Berthet-Bondets bought a sixteenth century house with caves underneath, and built a modern winery.

Vineyard holdings are quite broken up, with half in Château-Chalon and half in Côtes de Jura, and more or less equally divided between Chardonnay and Savagnin. There is 1 ha of Poulsard and Trousseau and a tiny parcel of Pinot Noir. The aim is to look for finesse rather than rusticity. Initially there was only wine, under voile in traditional manner, but now there is a Crémant (unusually characterful for the region), a red, and a range of both "classique" (modern) and "tradition" (oxidized under voile) white wines. The type of wine is stated only on the back label, as *ouillé* or *vinifié sous voile*.

The classique wines include Chardonnay or Savagnin from the Côtes de Jura; the oxidized wines are an assemblage of Savagnin and Chardonnay from Côtes du Jura (the Tradition cuvée), Savagnin from Côtes de Jura, and Vin Jaune from Château-Chalon. There is also a Vin de Paille and a Macvin. I find the oxidized styles more interesting than the classique, and the best wine by far is the Château-Chalon.

Domaine Jean Bourdy *

41 rue St. Vincent, 39140 Arlay	☏ +33 3 84 85 03 70
@ contact@domainebourdy.com	👤 Jean-Francois & Laura Bourdy
🌐 www.cavesjeanbourdy.com	◎ Arbois [map p. 98]
🧍 🏭 🍷 🛢 🍾 ⓘ 10 ha	🍾 Château-Chalon

This is surely one of the most, if not the most, traditional domains in the Jura. Jean-François Bourdy is the fifteenth generation. The house was originally just a kitchen and bedroom, and the sixteenth century caves below are still in use. The vineyards are in Arlay except for some in Château-Chalon. "We have documentation for the production methods for all the old wines, and we follow exactly the same procedures as a hundred years ago; no experimentation or new things," says Jean-François. Bottles have been kept since the eighteenth century, and the library now has 3,000 bottles; vintages for sale go back to the nineteenth century.

How many cuvées do you make, I asked? "We don't make cuvées. We make separate wines: red and white from the Côtes de Jura, Vin Jaune from Château-Chalon, and Vin de Paille, and Macvin, including one made by a (written) recipe from 1579 (which includes spices and herbs). The tradition in the Jura is to have an extended range, but there are no cuvées or vins de cépage."

The tradition at Bourdy is to keep wines for at least four years in old tonneaux before bottling; there are no young wines here. "Never, never, never any new oak: it would be an error because old oak is neutral." The red ("Our village is considered the leader for vin rouge") is traditional to the extent of cofermenting Pinot Noir, Poulsard, and Trousseau; the Côtes de Jura is Chardonnay; the Vin Jaune from Château-Chalon is the most concentrated of all the wines.

Domaine Dugois *

4 rue de La Mirode, 39600 Les Arsures	+33 3 84 66 03 41
@ daniel.dugois@wanadoo.fr	Philippe Dugois
www.vins-danieldugois.com	Arbois [map p. 97]
	Arbois, Trousseau Grevillière
11 ha; 60,000 btl	Arbois, Savagnin Auréoline

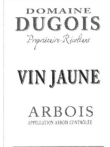

The domain started when Daniel Dugois bought 2 ha of vineyards and a house in Les Arsures. For the first few years the grapes were sold, and Daniel produced his first vintage in 1982. The domain has been expanded since then, but remains a family business, with Daniel's son, Philippe, joining him in 2003, and taking charge of the vineyards in 2013. White wines include Chardonnay in *ouillé* style, and Savagnin in both *ouillé* and sous voile styles, as well as Vin Jaune. There are also several cuvées of Trousseau and a Poulsard. The style here tends to subtlety: nothing is overdone. The Chardonnay is faintly savory, the Savagnin a little more so, with both showing a characteristic smooth texture. The Savagnin sous Voile offers a delicate expression of the oxidative style. The lead red wine is the Trousseau Grevillière, which comes from 60-year-old vines. All the wines are Arbois AOP.

Domaine Ganevat *

La Combe, 39190 Rotalier	+33 3 84 25 02 69
@ anne.ganevat@orange.fr	Anne Ganevat
	Côtes de Jura [map p. 96]
13 ha; 40,000 btl	Côtes de Jura, Grandes Teppes, Chardonnay

After working for eight years in Burgundy, Jean-François took over the domain in 1998. Ganevat's cellars run under a row of houses in the main street of a hamlet at the southern tip of the Jura. Extended little by little, the caves are old at one end, but run into a new extension. Vineyards are in many separate parcels. Jean-François has increased the size of the domain a little, and has adopted Burgundian methods for viticulture and vinification. Almost all wines are made in the modern *ouillé* style, but the occasional oxidized style (such as Cuvée de Pépé) is very fine.

The domain has all five cépages authorized for Côtes de Jura and produces many cuvées from different vineyards, typically around 35 each year. In addition, Jean-François has a reputation for rescuing little known indigenous varieties, which go into Vins de France. He grows 17 grape varieties altogether. The wines offer good expressions of varietal typicity, but I was not blown away by them in the way their reputation would have led me to expect, perhaps because all the wines in an extensive tasting were from barrel: they may just need more time to express themselves. Lees aging is unusually long.

Bottled wines develop a character of minerality and salinity after about four years that is not evident in barrel samples. Those I like best are the Chardonnays from limestone terroirs, which although matured in barriques, resemble unoaked Chablis, at their best perhaps richer and more concentrated. The reds taste sturdier than you would expect from the use of carbonic maceration.

Jean-François sold the domain in 2021 to Russian oligarch Dimitry Pumpyansky, whose son Alexander manages their wine holdings, including Prieuré de Saint-Jean de Bébian in the Languedoc. Six months later, when sanctions were imposed on Pumpyansky following the Russian invasion of Ukraine, Jean-François formed a company together with Benoit Pontenier, director of Prieuré Saint-Jean de Bébian, to buy back the estates.

Domaine Henri Maire

1 Place de la Liberté, 39600 Arbois (tasting room)	+33 3 84 66 12 34
En Boichailles, 39600 Arbois (cellars)	
client@henri-maire.fr	Thierry Schoepfer
www.henri-maire.fr	Arbois [map p. 97]
285 ha; 3,500,000 btl	Côtes de Jura Tradition, Chardonnay

The Maire family had been growing vines in the Jura since the seventeenth century, but it was Henri Maire, who inherited the estate in 1939, who built the domain into the largest in the Jura by purchasing vineyards through the 1950s. The domain accounts for 20% of production in the Jura, and for almost half of the Vin Jaune of Arbois. Henri was a master at marketing, and during the 1950s, the domain became famous for its Vin Fou, bottled in the old style before the completion of fermentation to retain some effervescence in the bottle.

The domain was inherited by his children in 2003, and in 2010 they sold it to an investment group in Luxembourg, who in turn sold it to Boisset of Burgundy at the start of 2015. "We had two problems when we bought it," an informant at Boisset says, "The stocks of old wines and the state of the vineyards." Boisset has started a program to improve the vineyards, and consider that it is now beginning to take effect. It is widely acknowledged that quality had been slipping, but with such extensive holdings there is evidently potential for Maire to become a major force again. Current wines, available in a wide range of styles, are respectable rather than outstanding, and can be found at the tasting room in the center of Arbois.

Domaine Macle   *

14 Rue de La Roche, 39210 Château-Chalon	✆ +33 3 84 85 21 85
@ maclel@wanadoo.fr	Laurent Macle
	Château-Chalon [map p. 98]
12 ha; 40,000 btl	Château-Chalon

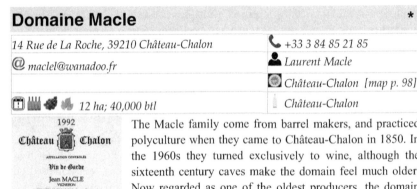

The Macle family come from barrel makers, and practiced polyculture when they came to Château-Chalon in 1850. In the 1960s they turned exclusively to wine, although the sixteenth century caves make the domain feel much older. Now regarded as one of the oldest producers, the domain has choice vineyard holdings, often on extremely steep slopes. Production here is focused exclusively on white wine; Jean Macle was regarded as one of the most knowledgeable producers of the oxidized style. He was followed by his son Laurent in 1995. The vineyards are divided into 8 ha of Chardonnay in Côtes de Jura and 4 ha of Savagnin in Château-Chalon. Alcoholic fermentation is followed by malolactic fermentation in cuve; then the wine is matured in barriques from Burgundy.

There are four wines: the Côtes de Jura (80% Chardonnay and 20% Savagnin), Château-Chalon, a Crémant, and Macvin. Jean Macle's reputation verged on reclusive, and with Madame Macle as the gatekeeper, it was always difficult to make appointments here, which may add to the mystique, but the domain is widely regarded as a reference point for Château-Chalon. Jean Macle's stated view was that Château-Chalon should not be drunk until 10 years after release, which is to say sixteen years after the vintage. The wine is then expected to last for a half century. All wines were produced in the traditional oxidized style until Laurent Macle introduced the first *ouillé* wine in 2007, showing a most elegant, refined style, albeit with only four barrels (1,000 bottles).

Domaine du Pélican *

Le Clos Saint Laurent, 16, rue de l'école, 39600 Montigny-lès-Arsures	✆ +33 3 80 21 61 75
@ info@domainedupelican.fr	👤 François Duvivier & Guillaume d'Angerville
🌐 www.domainedupelican.fr	Arbois [map p. 97]
🗓🍇🍷🍾📁 15 ha; 60,000 btl	Arbois Savagnin

The story goes that the Marquis d'Angerville, whose estate in Volnay makes mostly red wine but has branched out into white, was dining at a restaurant in Paris where he had instructed the sommelier to bring him a Chardonnay that did not come from Burgundy. He was so impressed with the wine that he thought the sommelier had made a mistake and brought him a Burgundy, but it turned out to be from the Jura. This led to a search for vineyards in the Jura, which led to the creation of Domaine du Pélican.

The domain started by purchasing the Château de Chavanes, which had a winery and a 5 ha biodynamic vineyard. "This was important for us because we work only in biodynamics in Volnay," says François Duvivier, who came from Marquis D'Angerville to run the estate. "Then we bought 5 ha in Grand Curoulet, it's one of the best places for Savagnin in Arbois, but the vineyard had been abandoned. Our most recent acquisition is from our neighbor Jacques Puffeney, who rented us his vineyards." (One of the most famous growers in Arbois, Jacques Puffeney is located a hundred yards up the street from Domaine du Pélican.)

Pélican makes only *ouillé* wines (in the modern, non-oxidative style). There are varietal Chardonnays and Savagnins, and a red blend of Poulsard, Trousseau and Pinot Noir, but no varietal Pinot Noir. "We don't want to produce a single Pinot Noir because it's an international variety, and me, I'm a Burgundian, so I believe Pinot Noir should come from Burgundy. We want to defend the local varieties, we will produce a varietal Trousseau in the future." All the wines are Arbois AOP.

"With Chardonnay we use 228 liter barrels and 15% new oak, with Savagnin there are larger containers and no new oak barrels. The Jura is always freshness and acidity and liveliness," François says. To start with there are only single cuvées of Chardonnay and Savagnin, but in the future there will be single-vineyard wines from lieu-dits Barbi and Grand Curoulet. "We've separated Barbi from the beginning, but up to now blended it, but now we understand it better and we are making a single-vineyard wine." It has greater depth and minerality than the Arbois blend, but still that typical freshness of the Jura. The other lieu-dit, Grand Curoulet, has an unusual exposure. "When I arrived, I asked the geologist, are you sure, this is facing north? He was right: it is great, but if you view the terroir with Burgundian eyes, you can't understand," says François. The Savagnin has a restrained sense of salinity and minerality, with the wines from the lieu-dits again showing more concentration.

The red blend is lively and fresh, very much in the style of Jura, with a little more weight than the varietal Poulsard, which is a nice summer quaffing wine. Domaine du Pélican is a work in progress. "If you come in 2022, you can taste our first Vin Jaune. Jacques Puffeney gave us some old barrels with the lees when he racked his 2009 and we put some Savagnin from 2015 in them."

Domaine Désiré Petit *

62 rue du Ploussard, 39600 Pupillin	☏ +33 3 84 66 01 20
@ contact@desirepetit.com	Damien Petit
⊕ www.desirepetit.com	Arbois Pupillin [map p. 97]
🗓 🏭 🍇 🚜	Arbois, Les Grandes Gardes, Trousseau
27 ha; 120,000 btl	Arbois Pupillin, Essencial Savagnin

The Petit family has lived in Pupillin for centuries, and the domain was created in 1932. Désiré handed it over to his sons, Gérard and Marcel, and today it is run by Marcel's son, Damien, and his sister Anne-Laure. Most of the vineyards are in the tiny appellation of Arbois Pupillin, on steep slopes above the village. The domain is converting to organic viticulture.

The whites are mostly in the *ouillé* style. Both Chardonnay and Savagnin tend to an elegant mineral style; the Cuvée Tradition is a blend of 70% Chardonnay with 30% Savagnin with some oxidative influences. "I want it to have an oxidative style but not too strong," says Damien.

The reds go through carbonic maceration, but retain a fresh, elegant style, with the purity of fruits that marks the house. "I'm a fan of Gamay," Damien says, "It's important to keep the old selections," He has found a 120-year-old plot of Gamay and is propagating it by selection massale; there will be a cuvée in about five years. Most of production is sold directly from the tasting room, with little available for export.

Domaine Ratte *

4 rue Jean Mermoz, 39601 Arbois	☏ +33 6 79 28 32 94
@ domaine.ratte@gmail.com	Michel-Henri Ratte
⊕ www.domaine-ratte.com	Arbois [map p. 97]
🗓 🏭 🍇 🚜 🍇	Arbois, Trousseau À La Dame
9 ha; 20,000 btl	Arbois, Melon d'Arbois

Formerly a grower, Michel-Henri Ratte left the cooperative in 2014 and started to produce his own wine with the 2015 vintage. This small family concern is run by Michel-Henri together with his wife François and son Quentin. They have started

with two whites and three reds, all in the Arbois appellation. There is one Chardonnay and one Savagnin, both in *ouillé* style—"we only have *ouillé* style," François explains, "because we have only just started and haven't had long enough yet to mature wines under voile."

The three reds are a Pinot Noir, a Trousseau À La Dame (the name refers to the cultivar, which is a rare variant with small clusters), and the Rubis cuvée, which is an unusual field blend of old vines of Trousseau, Poulsard, and Pinot Noir (planted as a mixed plot by François's grandfather more than eighty years ago). The whites are elegant and pure, the reds tend to be spicy, with Trousseau À La Dame showing the greatest depth, and unusual refinement for the variety. The domain has made a most promising start.

Domaine Rolet Père Et Fils *

11 Rue Hotel de Ville, 39600 Arbois	+33 3 84 66 00 05
@ rolet@wanadoo.fr	Pierre Rolet
www.rolet-arbois.com	Arbois [map p. 97]
☺ 🍇 🍷	Côtes de Jura, La Dent de Charnet, Chardonnay
65 ha; 300,000 btl	Arbois, Tradition

The estate was created in 1942 by Désiré Rolet, and in recent years was run by four siblings of the second generation, Bernard (viticulturalist), Guy (winemaker), Pierre and Éliane (marketing), until it was sold to Burgundian producer Domaines Devillard (who own Château de Chamirey) in 2018. Rolet is the second largest, and most extended, domain in the Jura, with vineyard holdings in many areas. It's a go-ahead operation with a tasting room in the center of the town of Arbois that offers almost all the wines. The modern facility includes stainless steel cuves and barriques, including some new wood, which are used depending on the cuvée. About half the vines are more than fifty years old; the others are regarded as young vines. Plantings are divided roughly equally between white and black varieties. There are vineyards in Arbois (at 36 ha comprising just over half), the Côtes de Jura (21 ha), and most recently an addition of 3 ha in l'Étoile.

There is a correspondingly large range of wines. The nine white wine cuvées comprise four Arbois, four Côtes du Jura, and an Étoile; they include Savagnin, and blends of Savagnin with Chardonnay, in both *ouillé* and oxidized styles. The Tradition cuvée is a blend of Chardonnay matured in *ouillé* style with Savagnin matured under voile, and is the most subtle of the blended cuvées, but all have quite intense Sherry-like character. The Côtes de Jura Savagnin offers a fine example of the style of Vin Jaune without the weight. The Étoile is pure Chardonnay. I like the Côtes de

Jura Chardonnay for the light savory edge, whereas the Harmonie cuvée from Arbois is heavier, reflecting its aging in new oak barriques.

The reds mostly come from Arbois, including separate monovarietal cuvées for Pinot Noir, Poulsard, and Trousseau, as well as Les Grandvaux (an equal blend of Pinot Noir and Poulsard), and a classic assemblage of all three. There are also several Crémants, as well as Vin Jaune and Vin de Paille from Arbois (and of course Macvin).

The style is relatively forceful, with spicy, nutty impressions for the *ouillé* Chardonnays, quite a strong oxidative influence for the Tradition cuvée, strong savory impressions for the Savagnin under voile, and a savory but subtle Vin Jaune. The wines are regarded as being among the most reliable of the Jura.

Domaine André et Mireille Tissot **

35 *Place de la Liberté, 39600 Arbois (shop)*	☎ +33 3 84 66 08 27
39600 *Montigny-lès-Arsures (cellars)*	
@ *contact@stephanetissot.com*	👤 *Stéphane Tissot*
🌐 *www.stephane-tissot.com*	📍 *Arbois* [map p. 97]
🏛 🍇 🍷 🚜 🛢 🍎 ⊘	🍾 *Arbois Pinot Noir, Sous La Tour*
50 *ha; 140,000 btl*	*Arbois Vin Jaune, La Vasée*
	Arbois Chardonnay, Les Bruyères

One of the most interesting producers in the Jura, Stéphane Tissot has built a great reputation since he took over the family domain a few years ago. The estate was called Domaine André et Mireille Tissot, but Stéphane's name was prominent on the label for years, until the label changed to Bénédicte & Stéphane Tissot. The domain started with 10 ha in 1950 with Stéphane's grandfather, who was a vigneron. The focus is on terroir. "Land is not expensive, although vines of quality cost more," Stéphane says. There are 42 ha in Arbois, 2 ha in Château-Chalon, and 6 ha on Côtes de Jura. Vineyards are a mix of large holdings and some very small parcels. All the vineyards are maintained by selection massale. Most of the wines come from the Arbois appellation.

Plantings are split equally between black and white grapes, but there is less red wine production because many of the black grapes, from the less interesting terroirs, go into Crémant, which is a quarter of production. The Indigène Crémant comes from the same base wine as the Brut Nature, but is fermented with indigenous instead of cultured yeast, giving a more flavorful impression.

Most of the white wine production is Chardonnay, which is vinified by parcel to give seven different cuvées. The house style offers a smoky, spicy introduction, following to a palate varying from mineral to more opulent, depending on the terroir, with a finish that tends to a savory impression in the direction of tarragon. La Mailloche is the richest—"This is always a little more rustic," says Stéphane. Les

107

Bruyères shows the domain's characteristic smokiness and spiciness—"This is completely different, with a very strong Jurassien expression," is how Stéphane describes it. And Le Clos de la Tour de Curon comes from vines replanted in 2002 at 12,000 plants per hectare, and achieves very low yields. With two year's élevage, this is always the most concentrated (and most alcoholic) of Tissot's whites. All the wines have a distinctive savory orientation. Savagnin Amphore is an orange wine.

The Arbois Savagnin, which spends 26 months under voile, is very savory, and more subtle than the Vin Jaune. La Vasée is the most mineral and savory of the three Vin Jaune cuvées, which are all very fine. "We look for finesse and elegance, there are many people who look for power," Stéphane says.

The reds are light and fresh, and at their best can show an earthy character. Pinot Noir is the most interesting, and the cuvée Sous La Tour is a fine example of the authentic style of Arbois, mineral and earthy, with some aging potential.

It's very lively at the domain, there are lots of experiments. One of Stéphane's most common words is experimentation, and if there's one word to describe Tissot, it's originality. Going round the vineyards or tasting with Stéphane is a whirlwind of activity. There is now a tasting room in the town of Arbois where some of the 36 cuvées of the domain can be tried.

Profiles of Important Estates

Château d'Arlay

4 Route de Proby, 39140 Arlay	📞 +33 3 84 85 04 22
@ contact@arlay.com	👤 Pierre-Armand de Laguiche
🌐 www.arlay.com	◉ Arbois [map p. 98]
🉑 🏭 🍇 🍂 🍇	22 ha; 45,000 btl

One of the oldest viticultural domains in France—wine has been made here since 1070—and a historic monument, built in 1774 to replace a convent built in 1650, the château itself is vast, and the cellars are all that remains of the convent. The present owners, the Laguiche family (known for their holdings in Montrachet) are descendants of the Comtesse de Lauraguais, for whom the château was built. It is set in an 8 ha landscaped park. The château and park can be visited all year. Alain de Laguiche has been in charge since the 1980s. The wines got a new lease when Philippe Soulard was brought in to take over winemaking in 2012. Vineyards on a base of gray marl face full south. Plantings are half black, with Pinot Noir dominant (80%). Whites are split more equally between Chardonnay and Savagnin. Vin Jaune is, of course, the flagship of the domain. Other local types include Vin de Paille and Macvin, both red and white. The Côtes de Jura start with the Corail cuvée, a throwback to a time when it was common to coferment all the varieties: Pinot Noir, Trousseau, Poulsard, Chardonnay, and Savagnin. The red La Réserve is a blend of all three red varieties: unusually it is also a blend across vintages. The domain is well known for its Pinot Noir, which is the largest production cuvée. The aging regime for reds was four years in old foudres for four years, but after a series of small vintages, it was changed to one year in a mix of barriques and 400-liter barrels. The change from long to shorter aging has given a fresher character to the wines. A Trousseau is aged in

108

cuve. Vin Blanc Tradition is a white with one third Savagnin and two thirds Chardonnay, cofermented, and then aged for three years in foudres that are topped up to keep a modern style. The Chardonnay cuvée à la Reine comes from a single parcel of old vines, planted in 1953 on clay soils; it ages on the lees in cuve.

Caveau de Bacchus

4 Rue Boutière, 39600 Montigny-lès-Arsures	📞 *+33 3 84 66 11 02*
@ *caveaubacchus39@gmail.com*	👤 *Vincent Aviet*
🌐 *caveaudebacchusearl.site-solocal.com*	◉ *Arbois [map p. 97]*
🚶 🏭 🍇 ☙	*5 ha; 24,000 btl*

Although the atmosphere seems touristic, this is a serious domain producing only still wine—no Macvin, no marc, no crémant. Lucien Aviet started making wine here in 1960, and his son Vincent started taking over from 1993. (The calligraphic labels say Lucien Aviet & Fils in larger type than Caveau de Bacchus, which refers to Lucien's nickname.) Wines under the Arbois appellation come from 18 separate small parcels. Production is split equally between red and white. The domain is known for its Trousseau, the Cuvée des Géologues. The Cuvée des Docteurs comes from a variant of Chardonnay called Maison à Queue Rouge (named for its red stalks), although regulations prevent the variety from being stated on the label. It is *ouillé* in the modern style. Almost the entire production is sold directly from the cellar door.

Domaine Benoît Badoz

3, Avenue de la Gare (shop>	📞 *+33 3 84 37 18 00*
19 Place des Déportés, 39800 Poligny (cellars)	
@ *contact@domaine-badoz.fr*	👤 *Benoît Badoz*
🌐 *www.domaine-badoz.fr*	◉ *Arbois [map p. 97]*
◐ 🏭 🍇 🛢 🍷 ∅	*10 ha; 100,000 btl*

The Badoz family has been making wine in Poligny since 1659 from its holding in the lieu-dit Roussots. Benoît, the tenth generation, took over from his father in 2003, introducing new cuvées and building a new, modern cellar. There is a wine shop just down the road in the town of Poligny. There are three Chardonnay cuvées under Côtes de Jura: the first is aged in steel, Les Roussots comes from specific parcels and ages in barriques, and Arrogance comes from the oldest vines and ages in barriques. These are the modern, *ouillé* style, as is the Savagnin cuvée Victoria, aged in steel. Tradition is a Chardonnay-Savagnin blend in the oxidized style, as is the Savagnin Côtes de Jura. Vin Jaune, Vin de Paille, and Macvin complete the range of whites. Reds from the traditional varieties are about a quarter of production. Crémant comes mostly from purchased grapes.

Domaine Baud Père Et Fils

222 Route de Voiteur, 39210 Le Vernois	📞 *+33 3 84 25 31 41*
@ *clementine@domainebaud.fr*	👤 *Clementine Baud*
🌐 *www.domainebaud.fr*	◉ *Arbois [map p. 98]*
🚶 🏭 🍇 ☙	*25 ha; 150,000 btl*

This is an old domain, dating from 1742, but fell into disrepair following phylloxera. René Baud, the 7th generation, started to reconstruct the vineyards in 1950, starting with just 4 ha. His sons Jean-Michel and Alain took over in 1978; and the 9th generation, Clémentine and Bastien (winemaker and viticulturalist) took over in 2016. Most of the vineyards (19 ha) are Côtes de Jura, and there are 3 ha each in Château Chalon and L'Étoile. Three quarters of production is white, and another 5% is Vin Jaune. Deux Grains de Paradis is a blend between tradition and modernity, with half from Savagnin aged under voile and half from Chardonnay aged in foudres. Les Prémices is AOP L'Étoile, Chardonnay aged in oak from barriques to foudres, in modern style. Cuvée Flor is a Chardonnay from the Côtes de Jura, aged in ouillé (modern) style, in vats. L'Un is Savagnin from Côtes de Jura, aged in barriques in traditional style. There are two wines in Vin Jaune style: Château Chalon and the cuvée Clavéline from Côtes de Jura, aged for the same 6 years as the Château Chalon. Reds include Poulsard, Ancéstrale (a Pinot Noir-Trousseau blend), and Trousseau.

Domaine de la Borde

Chemin des vignes 39600 Pupillin	+33 3 84 66 25 61
mareschal.julien@gmail.com	Julien Mareschal
www.domaine-de-la-borde.fr	Arbois Pupillin [map p. 97]
	5 ha; 20,000 btl

With a background in agriculture rather than winemaking, Julien Mareschal established his domain at Pupillin in 2003. Even though the domain is small, he has all the varieties of the Jura, and makes wines in both traditional and modern style. The reds are all varietals: Poulsard, Trousseau, and Pinot Noir. Poulsard Côte de Feule is made without any sulfur. Whites include Chardonnay and Savagnin, both under voile and ouillé, and also an unusual white from Poulsard. All the wines are named for individual parcels.

Les Bottes Rouges

10 rue du Lavoir, 39800 Abergement-le-Petit	
lesbottesrouges@free.fr	Jean-Baptiste Menigoz
7 ha; 25,000 btl	Arbois [map p. 97]

Jean-Baptiste Menigoz started making wine on the side from his job as a teacher, focusing on natural wine, until 2015 when he devoted himself to the domain together with his wife Jacqueline and partner Florien Kleine Snuverink, formerly a restaurant owner in Amsterdam. They started with 2.5 ha and now own vineyards in Abergement and Arbois (a few miles to the east). Wine are modern in style. Cuvées include Aléas (a Vin de France blend of Trousseau, Ploussard, and Pinot Noir vinified in fiberglass tanks), Castor (Vin de France, Chardonnay directly pressed into 400-liter barrels), Léon (Arbois Chardonnay fermented in foudre and aged in 400-liter barrels), and Album (Savagnin *Ouillé* from Arbois). There are several whites in Côtes de Jura, and some varietal reds from Arbois, La Pepée (Pinot Noir) and Gibus (Trousseau)

Domaine Bruyère-Houillon

| 24, rue du Ploussard, 39600 Pupillin | +33 6 84 28 40 14 |

110

@ renaud.bruyere22@orange.fr	👤 Renaud Bruyère
📅 🏭 🍇 🍂 🍵 4 ha; 9,000 btl	🔴 Arbois Pupillin [map p. 97]

Adeline Houillon and Renaud Bruyère started their domain in Pupillin in 2011 with less than a hectare. Adeline gained experience working with her brother Emmanuel at Domaine Overnoy (see profile); and Renaud worked first at Overnoy and then with Stéphane Tissot from 2007 to 2015. At one point they reached 5 ha, but then they cut back by a hectare. There are now 2.5 ha of white and 1.5 ha of red. The first parcel actually came from Stéphane Tissot, an old plot *complanté* (intermingled) with Chardonnay, Savagnin, and (a very little) Trousseau. This makes the cuvée Les Tourillons, essentially 80% Chardonnay and 20% Savagnin, in *ouillé* (modern style). There are cuvées from Chardonnay, Savagnin, Trousseau, and Poulsard. All the cuvées are ouillé, with winemaking following natural precepts.

Philippe Butin

21 rue de La Combe, 39210 Lavigny	📞 +33 3 84 25 36 26
@ ph.butin@wanadoo.fr	👤 Philippe Butin
🌐 philippe.butin.pagesperso-orange.fr	🔴 Côtes de Jura [map p. 98]
📅 🏭 🍇 🚜	6 ha

The family settled in Lavigny in 1920, and Philippe, who took over in 1980, is the third generation. Plantings are mostly white, with 4 ha of Chardonnay and Savagnin (including a tiny plot, only 0.15 ha, in Château-Chalon). The Chardonnay is *ouillé* (modern style), while Cuvée Spéciale is a blend of Chardonnay vinified modern style in cuve and Savagnin aged in barriques without topping up. There is a Vin Jaune under Côtes de Jura. The Château-Chalon ages for 8 years. Reds include Poulsard and Trousseau.

Domaine Cartaux Bougaud

5, Rue des Vignes, Juhans, 39140 Arlay	📞 +33 3 84 48 11 51
@ contact@vinscartaux.fr	👤 Sandrine & Sébastien Cartaux
🌐 www.vinscartaux.fr	🔴 Arbois [map p. 98]
🧍 🏭 🍇 🚜	15 ha; 65,000 btl

The domain was founded in 1973 with a few rows of vines, and planted some vineyards and made wine on a small scale until 1983, when it became a full-time occupation. In 1993, the second generation, Sébastien and his wife Nathalie, joined the domain. A cuverie was constructed in the vineyards at Arlay in 2001; the family also owns a medieval castle, the Château de Quintigny, where the wines are aged, and which is open for tastings and events in July and August. Vineyards are in appellations l'Etoile and Côtes de Jura. Under l'Etoile there are traditional cuvées of both Savagnin and Chardonnay, and a blend of coplanted varieties from the Paradis lieu-dit. Under Côtes de Jura there's a traditional Chardonnay and also a "ouillé" (nonoxidized) cuvée, Chardonnay Floral. There are also Vin Jaune, Vin de Paille, and some red cuvées (about a quarter of production).

Domaine des Cavarodes

28 grande rue, 39600 Cramans	📞 +33 6 22 74 96 70

111

@ contact@findandfund.com   👤 *Etienne Thiébaud*
⊕ domainedescavarodes.com   *Jura*

     5 ha; 54,000 btl

Etienne Thiébaud worked at the Domaine de la Tournelle before starting his own small domain in 2007. The property includes some small parcels of very old vines, 60-120-years old, just to the north of the border of the Arbois appellation (virtually at the border of the Jura AOP). These include some unusual varieties. Etienne is committed to natural winemaking and is considered a leader in the area. Very little or no sulfur is used during vinification, and none during aging or bottling. Reds are made by semi-carbonic maceration followed by aging in oak. There is a wide range for such a small domain. The red field blend from 10 or more varieties is an IGP Franche-Comté. The Arbois red St. Roch is a blend of the three principal varieties, Pinot Noir, Trousseau, and Poulsard, from a parcel of 50-year-old vines. Arbois Chardonnay is aged for 16 months in barriques in modern style (ouillé). There are reds from Poulsard and Trousseau.

Vins Jérôme Arnoux

23 Route de Villeneuve, 39600 Arbois (cellars)   📞 *+33 6 61 92 80 76*
5 rue de Bourgogne, 39600 Arbois (tastings)

@ *contact@jeromearnoux.com*   👤 *Jérôme Arnoux*
⊕ *www.jeromearnoux.com*   *Arbois [map p. 97]*

     20 ha; 160,000 btl

La Reine Jaune is a historic monument in Arbois, with cellars dating from 1322. Bénédicte and Stéphane Tissot took it over in 1997 when they started the negociant Cellier des Tiercelines. They sold it in 2014 to Jerôme Arnoux, who now makes wine under his own name. The Cave divides its wines into two lists: La Cave de Reine Jaune (negociant) and Les Cuvées Jérôme Arnoux (Domaine Chantemerle). There are cuvées in both modern and traditional style.

Domaine Philippe Chatillon

8 bis Rue du Collège, 39800 Poligny   📞 *+33 6 45 39 17 63*
@ *domainechatillon@gmail.com*   👤 *Philippe Chatillon*
⊕ *www.vins-philippechatillon.com*   *Côtes de Jura [map p. 97]*

     4 ha; 5,000 btl

Philippe Chatillon was the estate manager at Domaine de la Pinte (see profile) for eighteen years, until he left in 2013 to create his own domain. He has continued the same approach of organic and biodynamic viticulture. "I am organic, but also natural wine without any additions," he says. The wines are made in a seventeenth century cellar in Poligny, with a crystal harp and singing bowls used to generate sound waves to create 'bio-harmony'. His first vineyards were 2 ha consisting of plots of Savagnin, Melon à Queue Rouge, Gamay, and some old Pinot Noir and Chardonnay. Now there are almost 3 ha in Arbois and another 1.5 ha in Côtes de Jura. The Arbois cuvées include Savagnin in both modern and oxidized styles, and Pinot Noir. Amphore is a Savagnin from very ripe berries, harvested at the end of October, fermenting for five months in amphora before

112

pressing off and then spending another seven months aging in the amphora. Côtes de Jura includes cuvées of Savagnin, Pinot Noir, Chardonnay, and Melon à Queue Rouge. The Gamay is Vin de France.

Domaine Chevassu-Fassenet

Granges Bernard, 39210 Menétru-le-Vignoble	📞 *+33 6 89 86 89 06*
@ *mpchevassu@yahoo.fr*	👤 *Marie-Pierre Chevassu-Fassenet*
🗓️ 🏭 🍇 🌍 *5 ha*	🔴 *Château-Chalon [map p. 98]*

Denis Chevassu-Fassenet bred cattle, but acquired some vineyards in the 1980s. His daughter Marie-Pierre studied oenology in Dijon worked in New Zealand, and then returned to the negociant La Maison du Vigneron in Jura, before taking over the vineyards in 2008. Another sister now looks after the cows. The reds are Pinot Noir and Poulsard, aged in vat. A Chardonnay in modern style ages in foudre or demi-muids; a Côtes de Jura Savagnin comes from En Beaumont (near Château-Chalon), and there is also Château-Chalon.

Domaine des Bodines

Route de Dole, lieu-dit Les Bodines, 39600 Arbois	📞 *+33 3 84 66 05 23*
@ *domainedesbodines@gmail.com*	👤 *Emilie & Alexis Porteret*
🌐 *www.facebook.com/pages/Domaine-des-Bodines/205120372895760*	🔴 *Arbois [map p. 97]*
🗓️ 🏭 🍇 🍂 🍷 🍇 🚫	*4 ha; 17,000 btl*

Alexis Porteret worked at Domaine de la Tournelle (see profile) and Domaine de la Pinte (see profile) before setting up his own estate in 2010 with Emilie, who works at Chocolatier Hirsinger in Arbois when she is not at the estate. Alexis worked part time at the estate until 2016 when it became a full time occupation. The main plot of 3 ha is besides the house outside Arbois, and there's also a 1 ha plot at Poligny. Grapes ferment in a mix of fiberglass and stainless steel tanks before aging in barriques. There are Chardonnay and Savagnin in *ouillé* (modern) style, and the cuvée Maceration Savagnin, which spends up to 6 months on the skins. Reds include Pinot Noir and Trousseau, and Red Bulles is a Poulsatd pet-nat (semi-sparkling) cuvée. The focus is on natural wines, with no sulfites, fining, or filtration.

Domaine les Dolomies

40 Rue de l'Asile, 39230 Passenans	📞 *+33 3 84 44 98 25*
@ *contact@les-dolomies.com*	👤 *Céline Gormally*
🌐 *www.les-dolomies.com*	🔴 *Jura [map p. 98]*
🗓️ 🏭 🍇 🍂 🚫	*6 ha; 15,000 btl*

Céline Gormally is certainly enterprising. When she had the opportunity to buy some vineyards to start the domain but did not have enough cash, she leased out some vines to some 70 families, in effect forward-selling the wine. The domain expanded when she was able to buy some vineyards from Domaine Grand. Her husband, Steve, was able to join the domain on a full-time basis in 2016. The vineyards are mostly in Passenans or Frontenay, mostly planted between the 1960s and 1970s, so there is a high proportion of old vines. Individual cuvées are very small; there are four Chardonnays and five Savagins, all in *ouillé* (non-oxidized) style. The approach to winemaking is minimalist, with very low use of sulfur. Wines age in old barriques and some demi-muids.

Domaine Fumey-Chatelain

2, quartier Saint-Laurent, 39600 Montigny-lès-Arsures	📞 *+33 3 84 66 27 84*
@ *contact@fumeychatelain.fr*	👤 *Raphaël Fumey & Adeline Chatelain*
⊕ *fumeychatelain.fr*	🔴 *Arbois [map p. 97]*
	17 ha; 80,000 btl

The domain started by selling grapes from less than a hectare of vines. The move to producing wine came after a freeze in the Spring of 1991 destroyed almost all the grapes: vinification started with the little that was left, in borrowed premises. In 1999, they renovated an old farm to become the headquarters of the domain. Raphaël and Adeline's son Marin has now joined them after gaining experience making wine in the New World. There are several cuvées in oxidative style: Savagnin NM is an assemblage from several vintages, aged for 2-3 years *sous voile*, the vintage Savagnin ages for 5 years, and the vin jaune of course for 7 years. In nonoxidative style there are Savagnin Ouillé and Chardonnay, aged conventionally in barrique. There's also an intermediate blend, called Tradition, consisting of 70% Chardonnay aged conventionally in barrique for a year, and 30% Savagnin aged oxidatively for 3 years. They describe it as having the 'Jurassien DNA.'

Domaine Grand

139 Rue du Savagnin, 39230 Passenans	📞 *+33 3 84 85 28 88*
@ *contact@domaine-grand.com*	👤 *Nathalie & Emmanuel Grand*
⊕ *domaine-grand.plugwine.com*	🔴 *Côtes de Jura [map p. 98]*
	10 ha; 35,000 btl

In the center of the Côtes de Jura, the domain has been handed down in the same family since 1692, and was run by three brothers until 2015, when Emmanuel succeeded his father (one of the brothers). His wife Nathalie comes from Arbois. They reduced the vineyard area and converted to organic viticulture. They describe their wines as fruity, strong, and powerful. There is a full range of wines in all styles, including both modern and traditional. The traditional range includes Savagnin Vin de Voile and Vin Jaune from Côtes de Jura, and Château-Chalon (cuvée En Beaumont). There are also Crémant, Vin de Paille, and Macvin de Jura. Reds include Pinot Noir and Trousseau.

Domaine Hughes Béguet

1 Rue Bardenet, 39600 Mesnay	📞 *+33 3 84 66 26 39*
@ *patrice@hughesbeguet.com*	👤 *Patrice Béguet*
⊕ *www.hughesbeguet.com*	🔴 *Arbois [map p. 97]*
	4 ha; 13,000 btl

114

Patrice Béguet started as an IT consultant in Paris, obtained a wine diploma in Beaune in 2009, and then changed careers to buy vineyards in his home village in Arbois. The domain is by the church in the village of Mesnay, with vineyards at 300m altitude on the Les Corvées slope of Arbois AOP. Patrice is committed to biodynamics and to natural winemaking. The domaine started out with simple labels, and then switched to a reproduction of the label used by Patrice's grandfather for spirit made by distilling gentiane. Some of the cuvées have funky names: So True is Trousseau, Oh Yeah! is a *ouillé* (modern) Savagnin, and Straight No Chaser is Chardonnay. Orange Was The Color Of Her Dress is a Savagnin from long barrel maceration. A pet'nat (semi-sparkling wine) from Poulsard, is called Plouss' Mousse; a Poulsard dry red comes from Côte de Feule at Pupillin.85745

Nicolas Jacob

66 impasse du Ruisseau, 39570 Cesancey	📞 *+33 9 89 54 95 91*
@ *kkerry8@hotmail.fr*	👤 *Nicolas Jacob*
🚫 🍇 🍂 ⊘ *6 ha*	◉ *l'Etoile [map p. 96]*

Nicolas Jacob started in wine by working at Domaine Macle, the arch-traditional domain of the Jura, followed by a period at Domaine Ganevat. He bought his first hectare of vineyards at L'Etoile in 2015. In 2019 he bought a small winery at Cesancey, with 5 ha of vines in the area, plus another hectare back at Rotalier near Ganevat. Even with only a hectare, he followed the Ganevat model of micro-cuvées from different terroirs. He divides production of Chardonnay at L'Etoile into Là-Bas (the lower part of the slope) and Là-Haut)the upper part of the slope, typically aged a bit longer before release). These are *ouillé* (modern style). There is a small production (one barrel) of *sous voile* (oxidative style) from Là-Bas Chardonnay. Le Bas des Perrières is a 50:50 blend of Chardonnay and Savagnin aged in a 300-liter amphora. Reds include Pinot Noir and Cuvée X, from some old vines of unidentified variety, which is a Vin de France. Wines are made without sulfur, fining, or filtration.

Domaine Labet

14 Montée des Tilleuls, 39190 Rotalier	📞 *+33 3 84 25 11 13*
@ *domaine.labet@wanadoo.fr*	👤 *Charline, Julien & Romain Labet*
🔲 🏭 🍇 🍂 ⊘ *21 ha; 70,000 btl*	◉ *Côtes de Jura [map p. 96]*

Alain Labet ran the family domain of 10 ha (Domaine Labet) on conventional lines, and his son Julien set up his own small organic domain (Domaine Julien Labet or Les Vins de Julien) with 3 ha in 2003. When Alain retired in 2013, the two domains were united, and the single Domaine Labet is now run by Julien together with his brother and sister. At the southern end of the region, the wines are Côtes de Jura. There's a wide range of wines, enhanced by a focus on selections from individual parcels, with 12 whites in the *ouillé* style, and 6 reds. The domain continues to make the range of the old Domaine Labet, but following Julien's enthusiasm, is adding natural wines that are sulfur free.

Frédéric Lornet

l'Abbaye, 39600 Montigny-lès-Arsures	📞 *+33 3 84 37 45 10*
@ *frederic.lornet@orange.fr*	👤 *Frederic Lornet*

115

www.frederic-lornet.com | Arbois [map p. 97]
| 19 ha; 90,000 btl

The family were growing grapes when Frédéric Lornet persuaded his father to start estate bottling in 1974. With his domain located in the thirteenth century Abbaye de la Boutière, Frédéric became a pioneer in producing wines in the nonoxidative *ouillé* style, which he started in 1980. "Don't confuse oxidation and terroir," he says. The wines are mostly Arbois AOP. The Arbois Nature is Savagnin, while Arbois Chardonnay Les Messagelins comes from a single vineyard, both in *ouillé* style. There are all three red varieties, Poulsard, Trousseau, and Pinot Noir, made as single varietals. There is also Vin Jaune from both Arbois and Côtes de Jura.

Domaine des Marnes Blanches

Quartier les Carouges, 39190 Sainte Agnès	+33 3 84 25 19 66
contact@marnesblanches.com	Pauline & Géraud Fromont
www.marnesblanches.com	Côtes de Jura [map p. 96]
	12 ha; 45,000 btl

Pauline and Géraud Fromont met in wine school and started their domain soon after in 2006. Their first vineyard was in Cesancey (where the soil is the white marl for which the domain is named), and then they added Vincelles and Sainte-Agnès (where the soils are heavier, red marl), where they are based. They have an old farmhouse that they use for wines vinified sous voile (oxidatively) and a new cellar for *ouillé* (modern-style) wines. There's an unusual cuvée from 60-year-old vines of a local cultivar, Savagnin Muscaté, which is more aromatic. They also make wines from purchased grapes under the name Coup de Jus. Côtes de Jura reds are Trousseau and Poulsard.

Les Matheny

4 Rue de la Planche, 39600 Mathenay	+33 3 84 73 98 67
emeric.foleat53@gmail.com	Elise & Emeric Foléat
lesmatheny.fr	Arbois [map p. 97]
	4 ha

Emeric Foléat worked for Jacques Puffeny, the master of traditional winemaking in the Jura, for eight years before he started his own domain with his wife Elise in 2007. The domain is named for the village they both grew up in. This is a tiny domain by any measure, with plots in Arbois, Montigny-lès-Arsures, and Poligny, and the wine is made in a 400-year-old converted farmhouse. As you would expect from the Puffeny heritage, the approach is traditional: "we work as close as possible to what Nature offers us." Everything is vinified in barriques. The Arbois Chardonnay ages for three years, The Côtes de Jura Savagnin ages for five years under voile, and there is a Vin Jaune. Reds include Poulsard (aged three years in barrique) and a Pinot-Poulsard blend.

Domaine de Montbourgeau

| 53 rue de Montbourgeau, 39570 L'Étoile | +33 3 84 47 32 96 |
| domaine.montbourgeau@wanadoo.fr | Nicole Deriaux |

www.domaine-de-montbourgeau.fr l'Etoile [map p. 98]

11 ha; 50,000 btl

The family has been making wine since 1920, and Nicole Deriaux has been in charge for the past 25 years, now helped by her son César. The focus is on l'Étoile (8 ha) and on Chardonnay (70% of plantings). In traditional style, under voile, l'Étoile Blanc and Spéciale Cuvée are essentially Chardonnay with a small proportion of Savagnin, with the Cuvée Spéciale spending longer (4-5 years) before bottling. There is also a Savagnin and a Vin Jaune. There is the full range of wines, with Poulsard and Trousseau Côtes de Jura, sweet wine, Vin de Paille, Macvin, and Crémant.

Domaine Jean-Luc Mouillard

379 rue du Parron, 39230 Mantry	+33 3 84 25 94 30
domainemouillard@hotmail.fr	Jean-Luc Mouillard
www.domainemouillard.com	Jura [map p. 98]
	11 ha; 50,000 btl

Jean-Luc Mouillard's parents grew grapes that they sent to the cooperative, and Jean-Luc created the domain in 1991 after he qualified in oenology in Beaune. He bought a house with sixteenth century cellars in 1997 and constructed a winery in 2005. Vineyards are in three appellations: Château-Chalon, L'Etoile, and Côtes du Jura. There are two cuvées from Savagnin under Côtes de Jura, Le Curieux in nonoxidative style, and the Savagnin sous voile, aged for two and a half years under a layer of yeast. Bas de Chaux is a Chardonnay in nonoxidative style. L'Etoile is a blend of Chardonnay and Savagnin in oxidative style.

Maison Pierre Overnoy

32 rue du Ploussard, 39600 Pupillin	+33 3 84 66 24 27
emmanuel.houillon@wanadoo.fr	Anne & Emmanuel Houillon-Overnoy
6 ha; 12,000 btl	Arbois Pupillin [map p. 97]

Pierre Overnoy took over the family vineyards in 1968 and was a pioneer in the natural wine movement, especially in avoiding use of sulfur. A notable figure in the region, baking bread and producing honey as well as wine, he handed over the domain to his protégé Emmanuel Houillon, who worked with him from 1990 and took over winemaking in 2001, although Pierre is still present. (The wines are now labeled Maison Pierre Overnoy, mis en bouteille par Emmanuel Houillon.) Vineyards are equally divided between Savagnin, Chardonnay, and Poulsard. The red is made by semi-carbonic maceration, the whites are pressed immediately, but both are protected by a layer of carbon dioxide. Fermentation for the whites can be very slow. Wines age in barrels of various sizes, and essentially nothing else is done until bottling, except for topping up the Savagnin Ouillé.

Les Pieds sur Terre

8 rue Jacques Coittier, 39800 Poligny	+33 3 84 55 62 55
contact@vinlespiedssurterre.fr	Valentin Morel
www.vinlespiedssurterre.fr	Arbois [map p. 97]
	7 ha; 25,000 btl

Jean-Luc Morel ran the family estate under the name of Domaine Morel for thirty years before handing over in 2014 to his son Valentin, who returned from a position in the bureaucracy to take up winemaking, and changed the name to Les Pieds sur le Terre, reflecting a more modern approach with an interest in biodynamics. Valentin often uses 'nature' to describe his wines; sulfur is not usually added during vinification. Vineyards are all around Poligny. Two Chardonnay cuvées differ in vinification, with Saint-Savin fermented in stainless steel and then aged in demi-muids, while Les Trouillots ferments and ages in old barriques. Another Chardonnay, the Champ d'Aubert cuvée, is an orange wine. Savagnin comes in both modern (ouillé) style, and oxidized (sous voile). The reds, Poulsard, Trousseau, and Pinot Noir, are all destemmed, fermented in stainless steel, and then aged in the stainless steel.

Domaine Pignier

11 Place Rouget de L'isle, 39570 Montaigu	📞 *+33 3 84 24 24 30*
@ *contact@domaine-pignier.com*	🧍 *Jean-Etienne, Antoine, & Marie Florence Pignier*
🌐 *www.domaine-pignier.com*	🔘 *Jura [map p. 96]*
🗔 🏭 🍇 🚜 ◌	*15 ha; 60,000 btl*

Located in the southern part of the Côtes de Jura, Domaine Pignier is the sole producer in Montaigu, just south of Lons-le-Saunier. The family acquired the domain in 1794, when it was sold following the French Revolution. The present generation of siblings Jean-Etienne, Antoine and Marie-Florence Pignier took over in 1984 and expanded the domain, which has vineyards in two blind valleys on either side of the village. There's a full range of all the traditional wines, with Savagnin and Chardonnay both sous voile and ouillé, and all three red varieties, as well as the red Cuvée À Table Avec Léandre, which is a blend of 11 old varieties.

Domaine de la Pinte

Route de Lyon, 39600 Arbois (winery) *8 rue de l'Hôtel de Ville, 39600 Arbois (boutique)*	📞 *+33 3 84 66 06 47*
@ *contact@lapinte.fr*	🧍 *Emmanuelle Goydadin*
🌐 *www.lapinte.fr*	🔘 *Arbois [map p. 97]*
🧍 🏭 🍇 🚜 ◌	*34 ha; 90,000 btl*

When Roger Martin created the domain in 1953, he planted 14 ha of Savagnin, making La Pinte the largest domain devoted to the variety in the Jura. A geologist, he established the vineyards on a band of blue marl that runs through Arbois. The domain was expanded by his son, Pierre, with its vineyards still all in one large block near Pupillin. There is a tasting room in Arbois. Wines include a Savagnin-Chardonnay blend and an orange wine from Savagnin, as well as the regular Savagnin cuvées. The style is rather ripe and a little soft. I prefer the traditional wines, especially the Vin Jaune, to the *ouillé* wines.

Domaine des Ronces

9 Impasse du Rochet, 39190 Orbagna	📞 *+33 3 84 25 09 76*
@ *maziermichel@wanadoo.fr*	🧍 *Michel Mazier*

🌐 *www.domaine-des-ronces.sitew.com*   📍 *Côtes de Jura [map p. 96]*

7 ha; 20,000 btl

Georges Maier founded this domain in the southern part of the Jura in 1950 with just 1 ha of Chardonnay; his son Michel took over in 1986, and his grandson Kevin has been in charge since 2016. The range extends from wines in modern style to show in traditional oxidative style. Florale is a modern chardonnay, with no more than a faint hint of the oxidation of the Jura, but the Chardonnay-Savagnin blend of Cuvée Georges is far more powerful, distinctly oxidative in style, and very dry on finish with salty aromatics. It is hard for the reds to get away from the rustic style of the indigenous varieties, but the Trousseau is riper and richer than the Poulsard. The Pinot Noir is lighter but more elegant.

Domaine François Rousset-Martin

54 Rue du Moulin, 39210 Nevy-sur-Seille	📞 +33 3 84 85 20 40
@ *francoisrousset@wanadoo.fr*	👤 François Rousset-Martin
9 ha; 15,000 btl	📍 *Côtes de Jura [map p. 98]*

François grew up in Burgundy, where his father worked at the Hospices de Beaune, qualified as an oenologist, and in 2007 took over the family vineyards near Château-Chalon. Grapes had been sent to the cooperative, but François now vinifies and bottles most of production, producing the remarkable number of 20 cuvées from different plots, almost none over 1 ha. Terroirs vary among clay-limestone, clay-marl, and gray marl. Many of the vines are over 20 years old, many are more than 30- or 40-years, and there are some cuvées from really old vines: La Chaux from 65-year-old Chardonnay, Vignes aux Dames from 65-year-old Savagnin, both in non-oxidative style, and Puits Saint Pierre from 80-year old Savagnin, in a mixed style (6 months sous voile followed by 10 months being topped up). In whites, there are 7 non-oxidative (ouillé) wines, all aged in barriques, and 5 oxidized (sous voile) wines. Reds include Poulsard, Pinot Noir, and blends.

Domaine De La Touraize

7 Route De Villette, 39600 Arbois	📞 +33 6 83 41 74 60
@ *contact@domaine-touraize.fr*	👤 Héléana & André-Jean Morin
🌐 *www.domaine-touraize.fr*	📍 *Arbois [map p. 97]*
	13 ha; 30,000 btl

The family has been growing grapes for eight generations, since the seventeenth century. Andréa-Jean left the cooperative in 2009 to start producing his own wine. Vineyards are in Arbois, and there is a wide range of cuvées. Three Chardonnay cuvées come from different plots, vinified conventionally, with aging in barriques that are topped up. Les Moulins is a blend of two thirds Chardonnay with one third Savagnin, also vinified non-oxidatively. Savagnin Terres Bleues is also nonoxidative, while Savagnin Typé ages oxidatively *sous voile*, as of course does the Vin Jaune. There are also varietal reds from all three black varieties, Crémant, vin de paille, and Macvin.

Domaine de la Tournelle

5 Petite Place, 39600 Arbois	*+33 6 31 93 16 80*
domainedelatournelle@wanadoo.fr	*Evelyne Clairet*
www.domainedelatournelle.com	*Arbois [map p. 97]*
	9 ha; 40,000 btl

Pascal and Évelyne Clairet established this domain in 1991, producing exclusively Arbois with a bent towards natural wines, never chaptalized, with very little sulfur, and no filtration. After Pascal died, Evelyne continued to run the domain. Savagnin de Voile is the traditional cuvée, aged for three years in tonneaux. There is also a Vin Jaune. Fleur de Savagnin is in the *ouillé* style. There are three cuvées of Chardonnay in the *ouillé* style, with Terre de Gryphées coming from soil with more clay, Les Corvées sous Curon from more gravelly terroir, and Cul de Brey from calcareous terroir. In reds, Uva Arbosiana is Poulsard made by carbonic maceration, and Trousseau des Corvées is conventional. The Clairets have provided something of a training ground for younger producers, several of whom worked at Domaine de La Tournelle before striking out for themselves.

Savoie

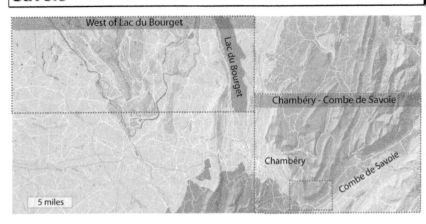

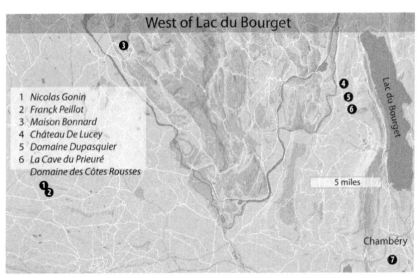

1 Nicolas Gonin
2 Franck Peillot
3 Maison Bonnard
4 Château De Lucey
5 Domaine Dupasquier
6 La Cave du Prieuré
  Domaine des Côtes Rousses

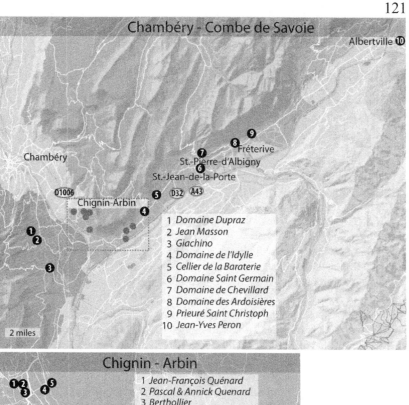

Profiles of Leading Estates

Domaine Louis Magnin   ★

90 Chemin Buis, 73800 Arbin	📞 *+33 4 79 84 12 12*
@ *louis.magnin@wanadoo.fr*	👤 *Louis Magnin*
🌐 *www.domainelouismagnin.fr*	*Arbin [map p. 121]*
🗓 🏭 🍇 🍷	*Arbin Mondeuse*
6 ha; 25,000 btl	*Chignin-Bergeron, Grand Orgue*

Louis and Béatrice Magnin have acquired a high reputation since taking over this family domain in Savoie in 1973, when it consisted of only 4 ha. Located near Montmélian, in the valley of the Combe de Savoie, right under the massive mountain of Bauges, vineyards are on steep slopes. The domain is certified organic but follows biodynamic principles. A new cave was constructed in 2006.

The wines represent the traditions of Savoie: in the whites are Roussette de Savoie, Vin de Savoie Jacquère, and Chignin-Bergeron (100% Roussanne); there is a special cuvée, Grand Orgue, from the two oldest parcels of Roussanne. The reds are the Vin de Savoie Gamay and Arbin Mondeuse. The two major cuvées of the house are the regular Mondeuse (more than half of production), and the Roussanne (around a third). Jacquère and Roussanne are vinified in stainless steel, while the Roussette uses a small proportion of 500 liter barrels.

There are three cuvées of Arbin Mondeuse: La Rouge, vinified in steel and then matured in a large old wooden fermenter; La Brova, matured in barriques; and the Vieilles Vignes: there is also a special cuvée, Tout un Monde, from the oldest Mondeuse vines. Occasionally there are sweet wines. The domain made its reputation for its specialty of producing Mondeuse as a serious wine, although the variety is inevitably on the rustic side, especially when young, but the top cuvées become more elegant if given time.

Profiles of Important Estates

Domaine des Ardoisières

Le Villard, 73250 Fréterive	📞 *+33 6 76 94 58 78*
@ *info@domainedesardoisieres.fr*	👤 *Brice Omont*
🌐 *www.domaine-des-ardoisieres.fr*	*Chignin [map p. 121]*
🗓 🏭 🍇 🍷 🔲	*13 ha; 30,000 btl*

Woods were cleared and the first vines were planted in 1998. The first harvest was in 2002. Brice Ormont joined the domain in 2005, and took over in 2010. Vineyards are on the slopes in two locations: at St. Pierre de Soucy near the winery, which is just off the main road through the valley, and farther north at Cevins. All the wines are IGP Vins des Allobroges. In reds, Améthyste is a blend of Persan and Mondeuse from Cevins; Argile is

123

a blend of Gamay, Mondeuse and Persan from St. Pierre de Soucy. In whites, Argile from St. Pierre de Soucy and Schiste from Cevins are blends of local varieties, while Quartz is varietal Altesse. Tasting here seems a bit commercial, focused on what is for sale; when I visited, the reds were exhausted so we tasted only the whites, all of which were faintly herbal and appley in a similar flavor spectrum.

Cellier de la Baraterie

La Baraterie, 73800 Cruet	📞 *+33 6 88 21 08 50*
@ *cellierdelabaraterie@gmail.com*	👤 *Julien Viana*
🌐 *www.cellierdelabaraterie.com*	🟢 *Vin de Savoie [map p. 121]*
🗓 🏭 🍇 🍂	*10 ha; 20,000 btl*

Julien Viana studied winema7-125king in Beaujolais and then in 2014 took over the 1 ha vineyard of a retiring vigneron in Cruet. Since then he has added vineyards in Saint-Jean-de-la-Porte and Arbin, producing wine from 5 ha and selling grapes to local winemakers from the other 5 ha. He has Jacquère, Altesse, and Malvoisie in whites, and Mondeuse, Gamay, and Pinot Noir in reds. Paroxysme is a blend of all three red varieties (40% each of Gamay and Pinot Noir, with 10% Mondeuse for backbone), fermented as whole clusters and aged in stainless steel; there are Mondeuse cuvées from Arbin and Saint-Jean-de-la-Porte, fermented as whole clusters and aged in stainless steel; and there are monovarietals of all three whites, with Jacquère and Malvoisie aged in stainless steel, and the Roussette de Savoie aged 20% in barriques.

Dominique Belluard

283, Route de Chevenaz, 74130 Ayze	📞 *+33 4 50 97 05 63*
@ *domainebelluard@wanadoo.fr*	👤 *Dominique Belluard*
🌐 *www.domainebelluard.fr*	🟢 *Ayse*
🗓 🏭 🍇 🚜 🍷 🍇	*10 ha; 70,000 btl*

Founded in 1947, in the far northeast of Savoie, the domain originally grew fruit trees, but was converted completely to viticulture by Dominique Belluard in 1988. The unique feature of the domain is that it grows Gringet (95% of plantings), an almost extinct white variety. The domaine has 10 ha of the 22 ha that are all that remain, all in Savoie-Ayse (only about 30 miles from Mont Blanc). Until Dominique starting growing it, Gringet was usually used only for sparkling wine. There are two cuvées of Gringet: Les Alpes comes from calcareous terroirs, and Le Feu (the top wine) comes from a local terroir of glacial sediments with iron-rich clay. Both go through malolactic fermentation before aging in concrete eggs. There are also two sparkling wines from Gringet, Mont Blanc Brut Zero and Les Perles de Mont Blanc. Aside from Gringet, there is Mondeuse en Amphore, aged as the name suggests. Sadly, Dominique died in 2021, and the domaine was sold to Vincent Ruiz, who wast he assistant to Frank Balthazar in Cornas. He renamed the estate Domaine du Gringet and produces only still wine.

Domaine Adrien Berlioz

2 place de l'ancien four, Hameau le Viviers, 73800 Chignin	📞 *+33 4 79 28 00 53*
@ *bureau.adrienberlioz@outlook.com*	👤 *Adrien Berlioz*
🗓 🏭 🍇 🍂 🍷 *8 ha; 30,000 btl*	🟢 *Chignin [map p. 121]*

124

Adrien Berlioz took over his family estate in 2006. (He is the cousin of Gilles Berlioz of Domaine Partagé). The estate is located near Chignon, at almost 400m altitude, with vineyards divided into thirteen different parcels. Yields are always low, around 25-35 hl/ha, which brings good density to the wines. The two monovarietal Roussannes are quite meaty. Raimpoumpou veers towards spicy with hints of apples, while Albinum is more restrained and earthy. Both are expressive of the character of Roussanne in Savoie. Two Mondeuse cuvées offer good illustrations of varietal typicity; cuvée Marie-Clothilde is earthier, but richer and more successful than cuvée Rosa (where alcohol is rather low). The monovarietal Persan, Cuvée Octavie, is the most elegant of the reds.

Maison Bonnard

78 rue de la Chapelle, Crept, 01470 Seillonnaz	📞 +33 6 83 79 66 34
@ bonnardfils@orange.fr	👤 Famille Bonnard
🌐 www.maisonbonnard.fr	🔵 Bugey [map p. 120]
🗓 🍷 🍇 🍂	16 ha; 80,000 btl

Roland and Frédéric Bonnard started to produce wine in 1988 from 1 ha of vines in their parents' farm. Now polyculture has turned to viticulture and the next generation, Romain and Anne-Sophie, are taking over. Vineyards are on the slopes of Montagnieu (with 30-70% gradients) in Bugey. Reds include Gamay, Pinot Noir, and Mondeuse; whites are Roussette and Chardonnay, and Romananche, a selection of the best barrels. There are also sparkling wines.

Jérémy Bricka

L'Usine de Mens, 308 rue Louis Rippert, 38710 Mens	📞 +33 6 64 33 83 20
@ jeremybricka@hotmail.com	👤 Jérémy Bricka
🌐 www.jeremybricka.fr	🔵 Savoie
🗓 🍷 🍇 🍂 🍂 🚫	5 ha; 10,000 btl

After qualifying in oenology, Jérémy Bricka spent 8 years managing Guigal's vineyards in the Rhône at St. Joseph and Hermitage. He founded a whisky distillery in 2011, and then in 2015 returned to wine by purchasing a parcel on steep slopes at 500-700m altitude in Isère (about 20 miles south of Grenoble). He planted indigenous varieties: Verdesse, Mondeuse Blanche and Noir, Altesse, Persan, Etraire de l'Aduï, and Douce Noire (Corbeau). The white grape Verdesse had been widely grown in the area, but had almost become extinct. It ages for 11 months in used demi-muids and is notable for high acidity and exotic aromas. The black grape Étraire de l'Auduï is a relative of another local variety, Persan, a member of the wider Syrah family. Douce Noire is the same as Argentina's Bonarda. Both are vinified using 25% whole clusters, before aging in demi-muids. The style is high altitude, with good acidity and brambly flavors.

Domaine de Chevillard

433, rue des Chevillard, 73250 Saint Pierre D'Albigny	📞 +33 6 33 01 12 21
@ domainedechevillard@yahoo.com	👤 Matthieu Goury
🌐 www.domainedechevillard.com	🔵 Savoie [map p. 121]
🚶 🍷 🍇 🍂 🚫	9 ha; 30,000 btl

125

After working as a chef, Matthieu Goury started making wine in 2013. His vineyards on the slopes of Saint-Jean de la Porte are planted about half with Mondeuse; other reds are Gamay and Pinot Noir. Jacquère provides most of the whites, with Altesse as the other significant variety. Reds are destemmed, ferment in concrete, and then age in old barriques; whites are pressed straight into barriques, and all except Altesse go through malolactic fermentation. Le Bérillon is the top red cuvée, from a parcel of Mondeuse planted in 1955. No sulfur is used except for a very small amount at bottling.

Domaine des Côtes Rousses

546 route de Villard Marin, 73290 La Motte-Servolex	📞 *+33 6 62 52 70 64*
@ *lescotesrousses@gmail.com*	👤 *Nicolas Ferrand*
🌐 *www.lescotesrousses.com*	🔘 *Vin de Savoie [map p. 120]*
🟥 🏭 🍇 🍂 🔲 🍇	*5 ha; 25,000 btl*

Nicolas Ferrand founded the domain in 2011. The winery is at his family farm, in stables that his grandparents used for cattle in La Motte-Servolex just to the west of Chambéry. The vineyards are almost all around the village of Saint Jean de la Porte (one of the Crus of Vin de Savoie), a few miles to the east of Chambéry: the domain takes its name from their red soils. Plantings are mostly the indigenous varieties of Jacquère and Altesse for whites, and Mondeuse for reds, although there are also some small plots of Chardonnay, Pinot Noir, and even Cabernet Sauvignon. There are two cuvées of Jacquère, La Pente aged 30% in barriques, and Armenaz aged entirely in barriques, Roussette de Savoie (Altesse), and a blend. There are three red Vins de Savoie from Mondeuse, starting with Les Montagnes Rousses, and then Saint-Jean-de-la-Porte, from older vines, aged in barriques, and the single-parcel Coteau de la Mort.

Denis et Didier Berthollier

Domaine La Combe Des Grand Vignes, 452 Route des Enrayons Le Viviers, 73800 Chignin	📞 *+33 4 79 28 11 75*
@ *contact@chignin.com*	👤 *Denis & Didier Berthollier*
🌐 *www.chignin.com*	🔘 *Chignin [map p. 121]*
🧍 🏭 🍇 🍂 ∅	*11 ha; 55,000 btl*

Founded in 1850, fifth generation brothers Denis and Didier took over in 1996. Broken up into many small plots, vineyards are on south-facing slopes about 10 km from Chambéry, and were extended in 2001 by planting some very steep slopes at the southern border that had been abandoned at the start of the twentieth century as too difficult to work. The estate was one of the first in Savoie to start bottling its own wines, in 1970. Denis and Didier started with appellation cuvées and introduced single-parcel cuvées in 2013. They are organic, but incorporate some elements of biodynamics, such as performing cellar operations according to the lunar cycle. Chignin has a Vieilles Vignes cuvée, and also the Argile sur Schiste cuvée, from a parcel of 70-year-old vines on clay over limestone. In Chignon Bergeron, the Exception cuvée is a blend of many parcels, and Les Salins is the southernmost plot, facing full south; both age in cuve, while cuvée St Anthelme ferments and ages in demi-muids.

126

Domaine Dupasquier

Aimavigne, 25 impasse du Vieux Pressoir, 73170 Jongieux	📞 *+33 4 79 44 02 23*
@ *domainedupasquier@orange.fr*	👤 *David & Véronique Dupasquier*
🌐 *domainedupasquier.over-blog.com*	🔵 *Jongieux [map p. 120]*
🚶 🏭 🍇 🌿	*15 ha; 80,000 btl*

Located a few miles to the west of Lac du Bourget, across from Aix-les-Bains on the eastern side, the domain is now in its fifth generation under David and his sister Véronique Dupasquier, although their father Noël is still involved. It lies in the picturesque hamlet of Aimavigne, just under the steep slopes of Marestal, one of the best crus in this part of Savoie (worked by hand because the slopes are too steep for tractors). Plantings are 60% white, including Chardonnay, Jacquère, and Roussette, including 1 ha in Marestal. Unlike most of the producers in the area, who age the wines only briefly in stainless steel, the Dupasquiers are committed to the traditional long aging in foudres. The top wine is the Roussette de Marestal, 100% varietal from 300m up a steep slope facing southwest. It ages in foudre for a year on the lees, followed by 18 months in bottle before release, and has long aging potential (older vintages are on the list at the Auberge Les Morainières, a local Michelin-starred restaurant.) There is also a Roussette de Savoie. Other wines include Jacquère and Chardonnay monovarietals and the red Gourmandaise blend, fermented from whole clusters of Gamay, Pinot Noir, and Mondeuse, as well as varietal wines from the individual black varieties.

Domaine Dupraz

Le Reposoir, 73190 Apremont	📞 *+33 6 17 51 39 35*
@ *vin@domainedupraz.com*	👤 *Marc, Jérémy & Maxime Dupraz*
🌐 *domainedupraz.com*	🔵 *Apremont [map p. 121]*
📅 🏭 🍇 🍃 🍇	*18 ha; 100,000 btl*

This family estate was founded in 1880: Marc Dupraz took over in 1980, followed by his sons Jérémy in 2011 and Maxime in 2020. Vineyards are on steep slopes at altitudes of 350-450m, south of Chambéry and west of Chignin. There are several cuvées of Jacquère, a Roussette de Savoie (Altesse), and Mondeuse. In the Jacquère whites, Cuvée de l'Apéro is a Vin Nature, Le Moulin comes from three parcels in Apremont, Les Terres Blanches comes from a parcel with atypical soils, a mix of clay, granite, and glacial terroir, planted in 1972, and Montracul comes from the oldest vines, planted in 1907, and given the longest (18 months) aging on the lees. Phoenix comes from vines planted in 1986 on the moraine glacier (rocky, glacial terroir) and ages in a concrete egg for 24 months. In addition to the Mondeuse, the red Phoenix comes from clay terroir and ages for 9 months in concrete eggs.

Domaine Finot

190 Impasse du Teura, 38190 Bernin	📞 *+33 6 84 95 21 44*
@ *thomas@domaine-finot.com*	👤 *Thomas Finot*
🌐 *www.domaine-finot.com*	🔵 *Savoie*
📅 🏭 🍇 🚜	*8 ha; 30,000 btl*

127

Thomas Finot established his domain in 2007 by resurrecting abandoned vineyards on the Coteaux du Gresivaudan in the area of Isère north of Grenoble. There are plantings of Verdesse (an almost extinct white variety) and the black varieties Persan and its relative Etraire de l'Aduï (based on a 70-year-old plot), as well as some more conventional Jacquère, Pinot Noir, and Chardonnay. New plantings are based on selection massale from the old vines. The domain also produces an entry-level range, Tracteur, with the red a blend of Gamay and Pinot Noir, a rosé from Gamay, and a white blend of Jacquère, Chasselas, and Chardonnay. In addition, Thomas produces Crozes-Hermitages from 1.8 ha that his family owns in the northern part of the area at Larnage.

Domaine Giachino

189, route des Côtes, 38530 Chapareillan	📞 +33 4 76 92 37 94
@ domaine-giachino@orange.fr	👤 Frédéric Giachino
🌐 www.domaine-giachino.fr	⬤ Roussette de Savoie [map p. 121]
🗓 🏭 🍇 🍂 🍇 ⊘	15 ha; 70,000 btl

The Giachinos are an old agricultural family, and began making wine when Frédéric inherited a small vineyard plot from his grandfather in 1988. Subsequently they gave up polyculture and turned exclusively to viticulture. Frédéric's brother David joined him at the estate in 2006. Two thirds of plantings are Jacquère; the rest are the indigenous grapes Mondeuse, Gamay, Persan, and Roussette. Wines are aged in cuve, except for Mondeuse, which ages in demi-muids (600l). Jacquère is used to make both still and sparkling wine. The range has been extended by the recent acquisition of Domaine du Prieuré Saint Christophe (see profile), which is managed by Frédéric's son, Clément.

Nicolas Gonin

945 route des Vignes, 38890 Saint Chef	📞 +33 6 10 39 25 15
@ nicogonin@wanadoo.fr	👤 Nicolas Gonin
🌐 www.vins-nicolas-gonin	⬤ IGP Isère [map p. 120]
🗓 🏭 🍇 🍂	5 ha; 25,000 btl

Nicolas Gonin struck out in a new direction in 2005 when he created his domain and took over his uncle's vineyards, located about thirty miles east of Lyon. He pulled out the existing plantings of Gamay, Pinot, and Chardonnay, replacing them with the old indigenous varieties of Mondeuse, Persan, and Mècle for blacks, and Altesse (Roussette), which is more than half the white plantings, Viognier, Verdesse, and Jacquère for whites. Wines are all labeled under the IGP Isère Balmes Dauphinoises. Nicolas studied oenology in Beaune, where he acquired his interest in old grape varieties, and then worked at Château Gilette in Sauternes, Domaine Tempier in Bandol, and Ridge Vineyards in California. He's Vice President of the Institute for Ampelography, and is campaigning to have varieties such as Mècle, Robin Noir, and Bia restored to the list of varieties that can be cultivated in France. "In fact, I'm the sole producer of Mècle, since the first harvest in 2017," Nicolas explains. "Although the Balmes Dauphinoises region is not mentioned in any wine atlas, my aim is to produce here at Saint Chef the best possible wine. I have planted only grape varieties where I have proof that they used to be cultivated locally." Vineyards are at 250-400m, on slopes of sandstone and gravel, facing south-southwest. Varietal red wines include Persan and Mondeuse, there is also a rosé from Mondeuse, and

128

whites include Altesse, Verdesse, and a blend of Altesse and Viognier (nominally not allowed). All the wines age in cuve.

France Gonzalvez

La Monette 73190 Apremont	📞 *+33 6 30 45 24 82*
@ *vindefrance.gonzalvez@hotmail.com*	👤 *France Gonzalvez*
⊕ *www.facebook.com/france.gonzalvez*	🔘 *Apremont [map p. 121]*
🗓️ 🏭 🍇 🛢️ 🍂 🍇	*2 ha; 30,000 btl*

France Gonzalvez got the wine bug when she worked during the 2004 harvest with Xavier Benier (see profile), a natural winemaker in the southern part of Beaujolais. She spent the next two years qualifying in oenology in Beaune, and made her first vintage in 2008 from a half hectare in Brouilly. The first few vintages were made in various rented spaces, until she was able to rent a facility in Blacé. By 2010 the vineyards had reached 2 ha and she was able to work full tine on the domain. As the vineyards grew, her husband Olivier joined her at the domain, which became a two person operation with plots in four neighboring villages. The range is supplemented by a small negociant activity. She has had some of the difficulties that all natural winemakers have with the AOP system, so the wines are sometimes labeled with the AOP and sometimes as Vin de France (and wines that are AOP may sometimes also have Vin de...France on the label as a jokey play on her name). Then she moved to Savoie, where she now produces about 10 cuvées, half red, half white. The whites include a Pet'Nat (lightly sparkling) from Jacquère, a Jacquère from Apremont, Roussette de Savoie, Chignin Bergeron, and Point de Chute, a Vin de Savoie from Apremont with increased skin contact. Reds include a Gamay made by semi-carbonic fermentation and aged in amphorae, a Pinot Noir from semi-carbonic fermentation, and a Mondeuse.

Domaine de l'Idylle

345 Rue croix de l'Ormaie, 73800 Cruet	📞 *+33 4 79 84 30 58*
@ *tiollier.idylle@wanadoo.fr*	👤 *François, Sylvain Tiollier*
⊕ *www.vin-savoie-idylle.fr*	🔘 *Vin de Savoie [map p. 121]*
🧍 🏭 🍇 ☕	*20 ha*

The domaine was founded in 1840 and remains in the hands of the founding family. Originally producing fruits as well as grapes, it focused on viticulture from the 1920s. Estate-bottling started in the 1940s. Brothers Philippe and François took over in 1975 and expanded the estate to its present size. A new underground cellar was built in 2010. Philippe's son Sylvain joined in 2011, and replaced Philippe when his father retired in 2017. The wines are Vins de Savoie, with whites from Jacquère and reds from Mondeuse, and also a Pinot Noir. Anne de Chypre is Roussette de Savoie.

Château De Lucey

292 route des Moulins, 73170 Lucey	📞 *+33 6 80 37 02 79*
@ *chateaudelucey@orange.fr*	👤 *Christophe Martin*
⊕ *www.chateaudelucey.com*	🔘 *Vin de Savoie [map p. 120]*
🗓️ 🏭 🍇 🍂	*7 ha; 25,000 btl*

129

A couple of miles to the west of Lac du Bourget, Château de Lucey originated as a stronghold in the thirteenth century, although the present château was mostly constructed in the nineteenth century. It has been in the hands of the same family since 1920. Owner Nicole Defforey planted the first vineyard, a hectare of Altesse, in 1993. Christophe Martin ahs been the winemaker since 2010. The vineyard now consists of several plots just east of the Rhône, at altitudes from 230-400m. Plantings are 80% Altesse (5 ha), with less than a hectare each of Mondeuse an Pinot Noir. The Altesse makes four cuvées under the label of AOP Roussette de Savoie, from plots with different terroirs. There is one cuvée each for Mondeuse and Pinot Noir, and a sparkling wine from Altesse.

Domaine Jean Masson et Fils

Lieu Dit Le Villard, 73190 Apremont	📞 *+33 6 12 58 32 26*
@ *dom.jeanmassonetfils@wanadoo.fr*	👤 *Jean-Claude Masson*
🌐 *domainemasson.com*	🔘 *Apremont [map p. 121]*
🚽 🏭 🍇 🌱	*10 ha; 60,000 btl*

Passed from father to son for five generations, the domain has been run by Jean-Claude Masson since 1984, today with his son Nicolas. Vineyards are all in the cru of Apremont (just west of Chignin), mostly planted with its one permitted variety, Jacquère. There are several cuvées from Apremont, and also a Roussette de Savoie from the other planted variety, Altesse. The three top cuvées from Apremont are the flagship Coeur d'Apremont, from parcels of 80-year-old vines, La Centenaire, from a parcel of 100-year old vines, and La Renversée, harvested at over-maturity from a single parcel.

Château de Mérande

Chemin de Mérande, 73800 Arbin	📞 *+33 6 83 15 05 88*
@ *domaine.genoux@wanadoo.fr*	👤 *André Genoux*
🌐 *www.domaine-genoux.fr*	🔘 *Arbin [map p. 121]*
🚶 🏭 🍇 🚜 ⭕ 🍇 ⌀	*12 ha; 70,000 btl*

Located in a medieval castle which they have renovated (the old domain of Château de Mérande), André and Daniel Genoux relaunched the family domain in 2001. and in 2008 were joined by their partner Yann Pernuit from Burgundy, although he later moved on to the Domaine Belluard. The domain is officially known as Domaine Genoux - Château de Mérande. More than half of plantings are Mondeuse; most of the rest is Roussanne or Altesse de Savoie. The focus is on natural wines, with minimal or zero use of sulfur. The domain is regarded as a reference point for Mondeuse, with La Belle Romaine from Arbin including whole bunch vinification, aged in cuve, Le Comte Rouge coming from old vines, all destemmed, aged in oak, and the single vineyard Saint-Jean-de-la-Porte.

Domaine Famille Montessuit

884 Route de Bonneville, 74130 Ayze	📞 *+33 6 16 63 91 68*
@ *famille.montessuit@orange.fr*	👤 *Nicolas Montessuit*
🌐 *www.facebook.com/ayze.montessuit*	🔘 *Ayse*
🚶 🏭 🍇 🚜	*9 ha; 55,000 btl*

130

Between Geneva and Mont Blanc, at an altitude of 450-550m, Ayze is not a place for the fainthearted to make wine: temperatures are below freezing for 120 days a year. Located in the center of the village, the Montessuit family has been making wine here for three generations, from vineyards on slopes of 40-50% facing south. André Montessuit established the domain, and his grandchildren Nicolas, Fabrice, Jacky, and Gilles took over in 2007. Many plantings are old, 75-115 years for the oldest vines. Soils are clay-limestone. This is one of the few places left where Gringet is grown (only about 20 ha remain), and it makes both a pétillant (lightly sparkling) wine and a still white wine, both under AOP Ayze.

Domaine Partagé Gilles Berlioz

Le Viviers, 73800 Chignin	📞 *+33 7 87 97 93 24*
@ *domainepartage@gillesberlioz.fr*	👤 *Maxime Gay*
🌐 *domainepartagegillesberlioz.fr*	⦿ *Chignin [map p. 121]*
🗓 ⚒ 🍇 🌶 🌓	*6 ha; 20,000 btl*

This tiny domain started when Gilles Berlioz inherited 0.8 ha in Chignin in 1990. A cousin of Adrien Berlioz at Domaine du Cellier des Cray, originally a landscaper, he is a self-taught vigneron. Committed to biodynamics, he works the vineyards with a horse. He produces Chignin and several single-vineyard wines from Chignin-Bergeron. Whites are mostly based on Roussanne and are three quarters of production. Jaja is a white based on Jacquère, La Deuse is a red based on Mondeuse, and Les Fripons and the flagship Les Filles are 100% Roussanne under Chignin-Bergeron. Wines age in cuve.

Franck Peillot

171 Route de Seillonnaz, Montagnieu, 01470	📞 *+33 4 74 36 71 56*
@ *famillepeillot@gmail.com*	👤 *Franck Peillot*
🧍 ⚒ 🍇 ♺ *7 ha; 45,000 btl*	⦿ *Bugey [map p. 120]*

The domain is just north of the northwest corner of Savoie, in the small appellation of Bugey. Franck Peillot is the fifth generation at this small family estate. He joined his father in 1985, when the domain was only 1.5 ha, and has built it up since then with many small parcels of old vines, most surrounded by woods or uncultivated areas. Many plots are extremely steep and can only be worked by hand. Because the area is basically at the junction between the Jura and the Rhône, it has terroirs varying from heavy clay to gravel and limestone. The grape varieties are similar to Savoie, and Franck's main plantings are Altesse for whites and Mondeuse for reds. "I like working with Altesse because it requires a lot of finesse," Franck says. "A great Altesse is essentially a wine that expresses great terroir. I label (my cuvée) as Altesse (although locally it is called Roussette) because you can make an Altesse-Chardonnay blend and call it Roussette. I want people to know that what you're drinking is 100% Altesse." There's no malolactic fermentation for the white. In reds, in addition to the Mondeuse, there is also a Pinot Noir (from 1 ha planted with the Pinot Droit cultivar). A sparkling wine, which is about half of production, comes from the less ripe grapes of Altesse, Chardonnay, and Mondeuse. Wines age in stainless steel or enameled tanks.

131

Jean-Yves Peron

Route du Fort du Mont, 73200, Albertville	
@ domaine.peron@gmail.com	👤 Jean-Yves Peron
🍇 2 ha; 40,000 btl	🍷 Vin de Savoie [map p. 121]

Jean-Yves Peron comes from Savoie. He studied oenology in Bordeaux in the 1990s and then worked with Thierry Allemand in Cornas followed by Bruno Schüller in Alsace. This gave him an interest in 'natural' wines. He returned to Savoie in 2004, starting with 2 ha, and making wine in the basement of the family farmhouse; his vineyards are farther south, close to Albertville, where he built a new cellar in 2017. Jean-Yves started a negociant activity in 2011 to allow some expansion. His vineyards are on schist, in many parcels at 350-550m altitude, with a high proportion of old vines, some 100-years old. Plantings initially were only Mondeuse for reds, and a more or less equal mix of Jacquère, Roussanne, and Altesse for whites. The reds are made by carbonic maceration, followed by pigeage and maceration with the skins. The reds age in old barriques for 12 months; the whites age in barriques or in 300-400-liter barrels for 6 months. The whites also have skin maceration and tend towards orange wines. Several of the wines have no added sulfur. They mostly do not follow appellation rules and are labeled as IGP Vin des Allobroges. The cuvée for which he is best known is the Mondeuse Champ Levat. The whites and other reds are mostly Vin de France. Cotillon des Dames is a blend of Jacquère and Altesse; Les Barrieux is a blend of Jacquère and Roussanne. Reflecting the extreme cool-climate conditions, alcohol is rarely above 12%. Under AOP Savoie, La Grande Journée is an orange wine from Altesse. All wines are made without sulfur.

La Cave du Prieuré

3447 Route des Vignobles, 73170 Jongieux	📞 +33 4 79 44 02 22
@ contact@caveduprieure.fr	👤 Noël & Pascal Barlet
🌐 www.caveduprieure.com	🍷 Savoie [map p. 120]
	27 ha; 200,000 btl

The domain is located in a fifteenth century priory, separated by Mont Charvez from Lac du Bourget a couple of miles to the east. Pascal and Noël Barlet are the fifth generation at this family domain, in the village of Jongieux at 350m altitude. Noël's son Julien is now the winemaker. Plantings are 55% red (including 10% for rosé) and 45% white. The large range includes all the varieties of the region: Altesse, Jacquère, Chardonnay in whites, and Gamay, Mondeuse, and Pinot Noir in reds. The top whites come from Cru Marestel, an area of 25 ha on Mont Charvez in the Roussette de Savoie AOP (meaning the wines are varietal Altesse). In addition to Marestal Tradition, cuvée La Favresse comes from a single parcel in the Cru. In reds, the top wines are Mondeuse Compostelle, and the Gamay-Pinot blend of La Chapelle, both vinified by semi-carbonic maceration, but then aged for 12 months in barriques.

Domaine du Prieuré Saint Christophe

Cave Dessous, 73250 Fréterive	📞 +33 4 79 28 62 10
@ michelgrisard@wanadoo.fr	👤 Clément Giachino
6 ha; 20,000 btl	🍷 Chignin [map p. 121]

132

Michel Grisard bought the vineyards in a rather dilapidated state, which he started to renovate in 1978 to create the domain. He left the family domain in 1983 to focus full time on his new domain, with the objective of "turning Mondeuse into a great wine." He also became well known for its efforts to rescue indigenous varieties. Vineyards are located on calcareous soils in Fréterive and clay-limestone in Arbin, with two thirds Mondeuse and a third Altesse. Michel retired in 2014, and the domain was taken over by Clément Giachino, son of Frédéric Giachino of Domaine Giachino (see profile). The wines continue to be labeled under the old domain. The Mondeuse has several days cold maceration before fermentation, grapes are not destemmed, and the wine ages in cuve for six months and then in barriques for a year.

Domaine André et Michel Quénard

1327 route du Coteau de Torméry, Torméry, 73800 Chignin	📞 *+33 4 79 28 12 75*
@ *am.quenard@orange.fr*	👤 *Guillaume Quénard*
🌐 *www.am-quenard.fr*	◉ *Chignin [map p. 121]*
🧍🏭🍇❄ *27 ha; 200,000 btl*	*Chignin-Bergeron, Les Terrasses*

Of the many Quénards in Savoie viticulture, Domaine André et Michel is one of the best known. This family domain dates from 1976, although winegrowing goes back four generations. The vineyards are on the steep terraced slopes of the Coteaux de Torméry, just above the town of Chignin, at elevations between 300m and 400m. The best vineyards face south and have slopes of up to 50%. The domain has eight cuvées, representing a complete range of red, white, and rosé, including all the cépages of the region. The Chignin and Chignin Vieilles Vignes come from Jacquère, Les Abymes is a cuvée from specific terroir, and there is a Roussette de Savoie. The main focus is on the three cuvées of Roussanne under the Chignin-Bergeron label. The basic Chignin-Bergeron is matured in stainless steel for eight months, and malolactic fermentation is blocked to ensure freshness; Les Terrasses (the 'cuvée prestige') comes from specific plots and has similar vinification; produced in very small quantities, Le Grand Rebossan has malolactic fermentation in barrique, and is aged in oak foudres. Red cuvées come from Pinot Noir, Gamay and Mondeuse; the rosé comes from an assemblage of Mondeuse with a little Gamay. There's a sweet wine from Pinot Gris, under the local name of Malvoisie, and a sparkling wine from Jacquère.

Domaine Jean-François Quénard

Lieu Dit Le Villard, 73800 Chignin	📞 *+33 4 79 28 13 39*
@ *j.francois.quenard@wanadoo.fr*	👤 *Jean Francois Quenard*
🌐 *www.jfquenard.com*	◉ *Chignin [map p. 121]*
📅🏭🍇🍷	*18 ha; 120,000 btl*

The estate has been handed from father to son since 1664; Jean-François took over in 1987 when it was only 5 ha, and enlarged the domain by renting more vineyards. Plantings are three quarters white. Under the local appellation, Chignin, there are two white cuvées of varietal Jacquère: Vers Les Alpes, (from 40-year-old vines), and the Vieilles Vignes, Anne de la Biguerne (from 65-year-old vines). From Chignin-Bergeron, there are two cuvées of Roussanne that age in cuve, Les Demoiselles, and Au Pied des Jours (from older vines), and a cuvée, Le Bergeron, that ages in barriques or demi-muids. The Mondeuse cuvées are AOP Savoie, with Terre Rouges the main cuvée, and Elisa coming from older vines. There is a Pinot Noir called La Baraterie.

Pascal et Annick Quenard

Le Villard, 73800 Chignin	📞 *+33 4 79 28 09 01*
@ *pascal.quenard.vin@wanadoo.fr*	👤 *Pascal Quenard*
🌐 *www.quenard-chignin-bergeron.com*	◉ *Chignin [map p. 121]*
📅 🏔 🍇 🥂 ◯ ⊘	*6 ha; 25,000 btl*

Pascal Quenard's father established the domain in 1987, and Pascal took over in 2010. Vineyards are on the slopes at Chignin. The range of whites starts with Chignin L'Epure (varietal Jacquère), and continues with several cuvées of Chignin-Bergeron (varietal Roussanne), including the 1903 Vieilles Vignes, now more than a century old. Reds includes a cuvée of Gamay and three cuvées of Mondeuse, including Lunatique, which is vinified without any addition of sulfur.

Domaine Saint-Germain

65 route de Miolans, 73250 Saint-Pierre-d'Albigny	📞 *+33 4 79 28 61 68*
@ *vinsstgermain1@aol.com*	👤 *Raphaël Saint-Germain*
🌐 *www.domainesaintgermain.com*	◉ *Savoie [map p. 121]*
📅 🏔 🍇 🥂	*12 ha; 65,000 btl*

Brothers Etienne and Raphaël Saint-Germain trained in viticulture and oenology and started bottling wine from their family vineyards in 1999. "Monovarietals are the classic sure values of the domain," they say. The range includes Roussette de Savoie, Roussanne (Chignin-Bergeron) two cuvées of Mondeuse, and Persan. Other cuvées are blends from Petite Arvine, Roussanne, Mondeuse Blanche, Viognier, Marsanne, and Altesse for whites, or Gamaret, Pinot Noir, Mondeuse, and Persan for reds. Altogether, the domain grows 21 different grape varieties, including ancient varieties from the region—the domain's plantings of Persan are 10% of all the Persan in France—and some from neighboring Switzerland (Petite Arvine and Gamaret), and makes 16 different cuvées. All wines age in vat.

Les Fils de Charles Trosset

280, Chemin des Moulins, 73800 Arbin	📞 *+33 6 82 36 82 62*
@ *lechaidesmoulins@gmail.com*	👤 *Louis Trosset*
📅 🏔 🍇 ☕ *2 ha; 16,000 btl*	◉ *Arbin [map p. 121]*

Louis and Joseph Trosset took over the family estate in 2000, with Joseph managing the vineyards and Louis making the wines. When Joseph retired, Louis continued alone, although the estate has now been reduced to less than 2 ha. The distinction of the estate is that it grows little but Mondeuse (2 ha: there are just 0.3 ha of Roussanne). Even so, with vinification by parcel there are several cuvées. With conventional fermentation, and aging in cuve, the wines are known for their longevity. A single white has been produced since 2010. Never large, production was cut by half by adverse weather conditions in 2021.

134

Les Vignes de Paradis

2, route des Gravannes, 74140 Douvaine	📞 +33 4 50 94 31 03
@ lesvignesdeparadis@orange.fr	👤 Dominique Lucas
🌐 www.les-vignes-de-paradis.fr	Vin de Savoie
🗓️ 👷 🍇 🚜 🍷	10 ha; 35,000 btl

About as far north as you can go in Savoie, Les Vignes de Paradis is located on slopes overlooking the French side of Lake Geneva. At one time Dominique Lucas was making wine both here and from a couple of hectares at the family estate in Pommard, but now he is devoted solely to Savoie. Dominique started in Savoie in 2008, partly to escape the restrictions of functioning within the AOP system in Burgundy, so not surprisingly his cuvées are under IGP Vins des Allobrogies and not under the local AOP of Crépy. He is an enthusiast for Chasselas, but also has planted small plots of Savagnin, Pinot Gris, and Chardonnay. Dominique calls himself an artisan vigneron, and true to the name, vinification occurs in a mix of barrels, amphora, and concrete eggs. The cuvées P'tit Coin de Paradis, Un Matin Face au Lac, and C de Marin are 100% Chasselas (and could have been labeled as AOP Crépy). C Chasselas sous Voile is made like a wine of the Jura. There are also varietal Savagnin and Pinot Gris cuvées.

Des Vins d'Envie

1145 rue de Mettanies, 38530 Pontcharra	📞 +33 6 23 12 82 82
@ desvinsdenvie@gmail.com	👤 Guillaume Lavie & Maxime Dancoine
🗓️ 👷 🛢️ 🍇 0 ha; 25,000 btl	Vin de Savoie [map p. 121]

This is a collaboration making wines by Guillaume Lavie (who makes wine under his label of Vins de la Vie at a small domain in Bugey) and Maxime Dancourt (who started the small Domaine de l'Aitonnement in 2010 after working at Louis Magnin). The wines of Vins d'Envie are produced at Domaine de l'Aitonnement. Vins d'Envie does not own any vines, but they work and harvest the vineyards. Envie D'être Sous Acide is a Vin de Savoie from 100% Jacquère. Envie de Chasse Au Dahut is a blend of Jacquère, Altesse, and Chardonnay. Envie de Tutoyer le Diable is a blend of Mondeuse, Gamay, and Pinot Noir. All the wines follow the precepts of natural winemaking. At Domaine de l'Aitonnement, Maxime produces Dark Side 'the hidden face of Mondeuse'), aged in 500-liter barrels and intended to be a *vin de garde*, and Solar 'the intense radiance of Altesse'), aged in 500-liter barrels, Genesis (Jacquère, aged in barriques), and Big Bang (a blend of Jacquère and Altesse aged in barriques and 400-liter barrels). Sulfur is used only in small amounts at bottling. All this from less than 1 ha of vineyards.

Glossary of French Wine Terms

Classification

There are three levels of classification, but their names have changed:

- *AOP* (Appellation d'Origine Protégée, formerly AOC or Appellation d'Origine Contrôlée) is the highest level of classification. AOPs are tightly regulated for which grape varieties can be planted and for various aspects of viticulture and vinification.

- *IGP* (Indication Géographique Protegée, formerly Vin de Pays) covers broader areas with more flexibility for planting grape varieties, and few or no restrictions on viticulture and vinification.

- *Vin de France* (formerly Vin de Table) is the lowest level of classification and allows complete freedom with regards to varieties, viticulture, and vinification.

- *INAO* is the regulatory authority for AOP and IGP wines.

Producers

- *Domaine* on a label means the wine is produced only from estate grapes (the vineyards may be owned or rented). *Château* in Bordeaux has the same meaning.

- *Maison* on the label means that the producer is a negociant who has purchased grapes (or wine).

- *Negociants* may purchase grapes and make wine or may purchase wine in bulk for bottling themselves. Some negociants also own vineyards.

- *Cooperatives* buy the grapes from their members and make the wine to sell under their own label.

Growers

- There is no word for winemaker in French. The closest would be *oenologue*, meaning a specialist in vinification; larger estates (especially in Bordeaux) may have consulting oenologues.

- A *vigneron* is a wine grower, who both grows grapes and makes wine.

- A *viticulteur* grows grapes but does not make wine.

- A *régisseur* is the estate manager at a larger property, and may encompass anything from general management to taking charge of viticulture or (commonly) vinification.

Viticulture

- There are three types of viticulture where use of conventional treatments (herbicides, insecticides, fertilizers, etc.) is restricted:

- *Bio* is organic viticulture; certification is by AB France (Agriculture Biologique).

- *Biodynamique* is biodynamic viticulture, certified by Demeter.

- *Lutte raisonnée* means sustainable viticulture (using treatments only when necessary). HVE (Haute Valeur Environmentale) is the best known certification.

- *Selection Massale* means that cuttings are taken from the best vines in a vineyard and then grafted on to rootstocks for replanting the vineyard.

136

- *Clonal selection* uses (commercially available) clones for replanting.
- *Vendange Vert* (green pruning) removes some berries during the season to reduce the yield.

Winemaking

- *Vendange entière* means that grapes are fermented as whole clusters.
- *Destemming* means that the grapes are taken off the stems and individual berries are put into the fermentation vat.
- *Vinification intégrale* for black grapes means the wine ferments in a barrique standing up open without an end piece. After fermentation, the end is inserted and the wine ages in the same barrique in which it was fermented.
- During fermentation of red wine, grape skins are pushed up to the surface to form a cap. There are three ways of dealing with it:
    o *Pigeage* (*Punch-down*) means using a plunger to push the cap into the fermenting wine.
    o *Remontage* (pump-over) means pumping up the fermenting wine from the bottom of the vat to spray over the cap.
    o *Délestage* (rack-and-return) means running the juice completely out of the tank, and then pouring it over the cap (which has fallen to the bottom of the vat)
- *Chaptalization* is the addition of sugar before or during fermentation. The sugar is converted into alcohol, so the result is to strengthen the alcoholic level of the wine, not to sweeten it.
- A *cuve* is a large vat of neutral material—old wood, concrete, or stainless steel.
- *Cuvaison* is the period a wine spends in contact with the grape skins.
- *Battonage* describes stirring up the wine when it is aging (usually) in cask.
- *Soutirage* (racking) transfers the wine (without the lees) from one barrique to another.
- *Élevage* is the aging of wine after fermentation has been completed.
- *Malo* is an abbreviation for malolactic fermentation, performed after the alcoholic fermentation. It reduces acidity, and is almost always done with red wines, and often for non-aromatic white wines.
- A *vin de garde* is a wine intended for long aging.

Aging in oak

- A *fût* (*de chêne*) is an oak barrel of unspecified size.
- A *barrique* (in Bordeaux or elsewhere) has 225 liters or 228 liters (called a *pièce* in Burgundy).
- *Tonneau* is an old term for a 900 liter container, sometimes used colloquially for containers larger than barriques, most often 500 or 600 liter.
- A *demi-muid* is a 600 liter barrel.
- A *foudre* is a large oak cask, round or oval, from 20-100 hl.

Sweet wines

- *Moelleux* is medium-sweet wine.
- *Liquoreux* is fully sweet dessert wine.

- *Doux* is sweet (usually not botrytized) still or sparkling wine.

- *Mutage* is addition of alcohol to stop fermentation and produce sweet wine. The style is called Vin Doux Naturel (VDN).

- *Passerillage* leaves grapes on the vine for an extended period so that sugar concentration is increased by desiccation.

- *Botrytis*, also known as *noble rot*, means grapes have been infected with the fungus Botrytis cinerea, which concentrates the juice and causes other changes.

138

Index of Estates by Rating

3 star

Château des Jacques

2 star

Domaine Jules Desjourneys
Domaine Jean Foillard
Domaine Paul Janin et Fils
Domaine Marcel Lapierre
Yvon Métras
Julien Sunier
Domaine André et Mireille Tissot

1 star

Domaine David-Beaupère
Domaine Berthet-Bondet
Domaine Jean Bourdy
Domaine du Clos du Fief
Domaine Louis et Claude Desvignes
Georges Duboeuf
Domaine Dugois
Domaine Ganevat
Domaine Mee Godard
Domaine de la Grand'Cour
Domaine de la Grosse Pierre
Domaine Jean-Claude Lapalu
Domaine Macle
Domaine Louis Magnin
Château du Moulin-à-Vent
Domaine du Pélican
Domaine Désiré Petit
Maison D. Piron
Domaine Ratte
Domaine Coudert Clos de La Roilette
Domaine Rolet Père Et Fils
Domaine des Souchons
Domaine des Terres Dorées

Index of Organic and Biodynamic Estates

Domaine des Ardoisières
Château d'Arlay
Château des Bachelards
Domaine Benoît Badoz
Cellier de la Baraterie
Domaine David-Beaupère
Dominique Belluard
Xavier Benier
Domaine Adrien Berlioz
Frédéric Berne
Domaine Berthet-Bondet
Yann Bertrand
Maison Bonnard
Domaine de la Bonne Tonne
Domaine de la Borde
Les Bottes Rouges
Domaine Jean Bourdy
Jérémy Bricka
Domaine Bruyère-Houillon
Domaine Joseph Burrier
Domaine les Capréoles
Domaine des Cavarodes
Vins Jérôme Arnoux
Joseph Chamonard
Domaine Chasselay
Domaine Philippe Chatillon
Nicolas Chemarin
Domaine de Chevillard
Domaine Raphaël Chopin
Clos de Mez
Domaine de Colette
Domaine Damien Coquelet
Domaine des Côtes Rousses
Les Côtes de la Molière
Bonnet Cotton
Denis et Didier Berthollier
Domaine des Bodines
Georges et Ghislaine Descombes
Domaine Jules Desjourneys
Domaine Louis et Claude Desvignes
Domaine les Dolomies
Domaine Anne-Sophie Dubois
Domaine Jean-Paul Dubost
Laurence et Rémi Dufaitre
Julien Duport
Domaine Dupraz
Domaine Dupré Goujon
Domaine de Fa
Domaine Jean Foillard
Domaine Fumey-Chatelain
Domaine Ganevat
Domaine Giachino
Château des Gimarets

Domaine Mee Godard
Nicolas Gonin
France Gonzalvez
Domaine Grand
Domaine de la Grand'Cour
Domaine Château de Grand Pré
Château Grange Cochard
Domaine de la Grosse Pierre
Michel Guignier
Domaine Céline & Nicolas Hirsch
Domaine Grégoire Hoppenot
Domaine Hughes Béguet
Nicolas Jacob
Château de Juliénas
Domaine Labet
Domaine Lafarge-Vial
Domaine Jean-Claude Lapalu
Domaine Marcel Lapierre
Château de Lavernette
Domaine Léonis
Thibault Liger-Belair
Château De Lucey
Domaine Macle
Domaine Louis Magnin
Domaine des Marnes Blanches
Domaine des Marrans
Château de Mérande
Yvon Métras
Domaine Jean-Luc Mouillard
Maison Pierre Overnoy
Domaine Partagé Gilles Berlioz
Domaine du Pélican
Jean-Yves Peron
Domaine Désiré Petit
Les Pieds sur Terre
Roland Pignard
Domaine Pignier
Domaine de la Pinte
Château de Poncié
Domaine du Prieuré Saint Christophe
Domaine Jean-François Quénard
Pascal et Annick Quénard
Domaine Ratte
Domaine Richard Rottiers
Domaine Roches Bleues
Domaine Romanesca
Domaine des Ronces
Domaine François Rousset-Martin
Domaine Ruet
Domaine Saint-Germain
Julien Sunier
Anthony Thévenet
Charly Thévenet

140

Jean-Paul Thévenet
Domaine Thillardon
Château Thivin
Domaine André et Mireille Tissot
Domaine De La Touraize
Domaine de la Tournelle
Les Vignes de Paradis
Des Vins d'Envie

Producers Making Natural Wines or Wines With No Sulfur

Château d'Arlay
Domaine Benoît Badoz
Domaine Baud Père Et Fils
Domaine David-Beaupère
Domaine Bel Avenir
Dominique Belluard
Xavier Benier
Domaine Des Billards
Domaine de la Bonne Tonne
Domaine de la Borde
Les Bottes Rouges
Guy Breton
Jérémy Bricka
Domaine des Cavarodes
Domaine Chasselay
Domaine Philippe Chatillon
Nicolas Chemarin
Domaine de Chênepierre
Domaine de Chevillard
Domaine des Côtes Rousses
Les Côtes de la Molière
Denis et Didier Berthollier
Domaine des Bodines
Georges et Ghislaine Descombes
Domaine les Dolomies
Domaine Anne-Sophie Dubois
Domaine Jean-Paul Dubost
Laurence et Rémi Dufaitre
Domaine Dupraz
Domaine Le Fagolet
Domaine Jean Foillard
Domaine Ganevat
Domaine Giachino
Château des Gimarets
France Gonzalvez
Domaine de la Grand'Cour
Michel Guignier
Domaine Hughes Béguet
Nicolas Jacob
Château de Javernand

Château de Juliénas
Domaine Labet
Domaine Jean-Claude Lapalu
Domaine Marcel Lapierre
Domaine Léonis
Thibault Liger-Belair
Domaine Macle
Château de Mérande
Yvon Métras
Maison Pierre Overnoy
Christophe Pacalet
Domaine Gilles Paris
Jean-Yves Peron
Les Pieds sur Terre
Château de Pierreux
Domaine Des Pins
Pascal et Annick Quenard
Domaine Ratte
Julien Sunier
Anthony Thévenet
Charly Thévenet
Jean-Paul Thévenet
Domaine Thillardon
Domaine de Thulon
Domaine André et Mireille Tissot
Domaine de la Tournelle

Index of Estates by Appellation

Apremont
Domaine Dupraz
France Gonzalvez
Domaine Jean Masson et Fils
Arbin
Domaine Louis Magnin
Château de Mérande
Les Fils de Charles Trosset
Arbois
Château d'Arlay
Caveau de Bacchus
Domaine Benoît Badoz
Domaine Baud Père Et Fils
Les Bottes Rouges
Domaine Jean Bourdy
Domaine Cartaux Bougaud
Vins Jérôme Arnoux
Domaine des Bodines
Domaine Dugois
Domaine Fumey-Chatelain
Domaine Henri Maire
Domaine Hughes Béguet
Frédéric Lornet
Les Matheny
Domaine du Pélican
Les Pieds sur Terre
Domaine de la Pinte
Domaine Ratte
Domaine Rolet Père Et Fils
Domaine André et Mireille Tissot
Domaine De La Touraize
Domaine de la Tournelle
Arbois Pupillin
Domaine de la Borde
Domaine Bruyère-Houillon
Maison Pierre Overnoy
Domaine Désiré Petit
Ayse
Dominique Belluard
Domaine Famille Montessuit
Beaujolais
Xavier Benier
Le Bourlay
Domaine Chasselay
Domaine Damien Coquelet
Les Côtes de la Molière
Henry Fessy
Domaine Saint-Cyr
Domaine des Terres Dorées
Beaujolais Villages
Nicolas Chemarin
Domaines Chermette
Laurence et Rémi Dufaitre
Domaine Le Fagolet

Château de Lavernette
Domaine de la Madone Le Perréon
Domaine Manoir du Carra
Domaine des Nugues
Château des Ravatys
Brouilly
Château de La Chaize
Bonnet Cotton
Julien Duport
Domaine Dupré Goujon
Domaine des Fournelles
Domaine Jean-Claude Lapalu
Domaine Laurent Martray
Christophe Pacalet
Robert Perroud
Château de Pierreux
Domaine Roches Bleues
Domaine Ruet
Château Thivin
Château des Tours
Bugey
Maison Bonnard
Franck Peillot
Château-Chalon
Domaine Berthet-Bondet
Domaine Chevassu-Fassenet
Domaine Macle
Chénas
Pascal Aufranc
Domaine de Chênepierre
Domaine du Granit
Domaine Céline & Nicolas Hirsch
Thibault Liger-Belair
Domaine Thillardon
Chignin
Domaine des Ardoisières
Domaine Adrien Berlioz
Denis et Didier Berthollier
Domaine Partagé Gilles Berlioz
Domaine du Prieuré Saint Christophe
Domaine André et Michel Quénard
Domaine Jean-François Quénard
Pascal et Annick Quenard
Chiroubles
Domaine de la Combe Au Loup
Domaine de la Grosse Pierre
Château de Javernand
Château de Raousset
Côte de Brouilly
Domaine de la Voûte des Crozes
Côtes de Jura
Philippe Butin
Domaine Philippe Chatillon
Domaine Ganevat

142

Domaine Grand
Domaine Labet
Domaine des Marnes Blanches
Domaine des Ronces
Domaine François Rousset-Martin

Fleurie

Château des Bachelards
Yann Bertrand
Domaine Joseph Burrier
Domaine Chignard
Clos de Mez
Domaine Anne-Sophie Dubois
Domaine de la Grand'Cour
Domaine Château de Grand Pré
Domaine Grégoire Hoppenot
Domaine Lafarge-Vial
Domaine des Marrans
Domaine Métrat et Fils
Domaine Gilles Paris
Château de Poncié
Domaine Coudert Clos de La Roilette
Domaine Romanesca

IGP Isère

Nicolas Gonin

Jongieux

Domaine Dupasquier

Juliénas

Domaine David-Beaupère
Domaine de Boischampt
Domaine des Chers
Domaine du Clos du Fief
Château de Juliénas
Domaine Laurent Perrachon et fils

Jura

Domaine des Cavarodes
Domaine les Dolomies
Domaine Jean-Luc Mouillard
Domaine Pignier

l'Etoile

Nicolas Jacob
Domaine de Montbourgeau

Morgon

Vignoble Arnaud Aucoeur
Domaine de la Bonne Tonne
Domaine Daniel Bouland
Guy Breton
Gérard Brisson
Jean-Marc Burgaud
Joseph Chamonard
Domaine de la Chaponne
Georges et Ghislaine Descombes
Domaine Louis et Claude Desvignes
Domaine Jean Foillard
Domaine Mee Godard
Château Grange Cochard
Michel Guignier

Domaine Marcel Lapierre
Domaine Léonis
Domaine des Montillets
Domaine Passot Collonge
Roland Pignard
Maison D. Piron
Domaine des Souchons
Julien Sunier
Anthony Thévenet
Charly Thévenet
Jean-Paul Thévenet

Moulin-à-Vent

Domaine Bel Avenir
Domaine Des Billards
Château Bonnet
Domaine Jules Desjourneys
Domaine Diochon
Georges Duboeuf
Château des Gimarets
Château des Jacques
Domaine Paul Janin et Fils
Domaine Labruyère
Yvon Métras
Château du Moulin-à-Vent
Maison Le Nid
Domaine des Pierres
Domaine Richard Rottiers

Régnié

Frédéric Berne
Domaine les Capréoles
Domaine Raphaël Chopin
Domaine de Colette
Gilles Copéret
Domaine Jean-Paul Dubost
Domaine Rochette
Domaine de Thulon

Roussette de Savoie

Domaine Giachino

Saint Amour

Domaine de Fa
Domaine Hamet-Spay
Domaine Des Pins
Domaine de la Pirolette

Savoie

Jérémy Bricka
Domaine de Chevillard
Domaine Finot
La Cave du Prieuré
Domaine Saint-Germain

Vin de Savoie

Cellier de la Baraterie
Domaine des Côtes Rousses
Domaine de l'Idylle
Château De Lucey
Jean-Yves Peron
Les Vignes de Paradis
Des Vins d'Envie

Index of Estates by Name

Domaine des Ardoisières, 122
Château d'Arlay, 27, 107
Vignoble Arnaud Aucoeur, 59
Pascal Aufranc, 59
Caveau de Bacchus, 108
Château des Bachelards, 60
Domaine Benoît Badoz, 108
Cellier de la Baraterie, 123
Domaine Baud Père Et Fils, 108
Domaine David-Beaupère, 20, 42
Domaine Bel Avenir, 60
Dominique Belluard, 123
Xavier Benier, 61
Domaine Adrien Berlioz, 123
Frédéric Berne, 61
Domaine Berthet-Bondet, 24, 27, 99
Yann Bertrand, 61
Domaine Des Billards, 62
Domaine de Boischampt, 62
Maison Bonnard, 124
Domaine de la Bonne Tonne, 63
Château Bonnet, 63
Domaine de la Borde, 109
Les Bottes Rouges, 109
Domaine Daniel Bouland, 64
Domaine Jean Bourdy, 27, 99
Le Bourlay, 64
Guy Breton, 18, 64
Jérémy Bricka, 124
Gérard Brisson, 65
Domaine Bruyère-Houillon, 109
Jean-Marc Burgaud, 18, 65
Domaine Joseph Burrier, 65
Philippe Butin, 110
Domaine les Capréoles, 66
Domaine Cartaux Bougaud, 110
Domaine des Cavarodes, 110
Vins Jérôme Arnoux, 111
Château de La Chaize, 66
Joseph Chamonard, 18, 67
Domaine de la Chaponne, 18, 67
Domaine Chasselay, 67
Domaine Philippe Chatillon, 111
Nicolas Chemarin, 68
Domaine de Chênepierre, 68
Domaines Chermette, 69
Domaine des Chers, 69
Domaine Chevassu-Fassenet, 112
Domaine de Chevillard, 124
Domaine Chignard, 18, 69
Domaine Raphaël Chopin, 70
Clos de Mez, 70
Domaine du Clos du Fief, 18, 19, 42

Domaine de Colette, 70
Domaine de la Combe Au Loup, 71
Gilles Copéret, 71
Domaine Damien Coquelet, 18, 72
Domaine des Côtes Rousses, 125
Les Côtes de la Molière, 72
Bonnet Cotton, 72
Denis et Didier Berthollier, 125
Domaine des Bodines, 112
Georges et Ghislaine Descombes, 73
Domaine Jules Desjourneys, 18, 43
Domaine Louis et Claude Desvignes, 18, 19, 44
Domaine Diochon, 18, 73
Domaine les Dolomies, 112
Georges Duboeuf, 1, 5, 8, 9, 15, 19, 45
Domaine Anne-Sophie Dubois, 73
Domaine Jean-Paul Dubost, 74
Laurence et Rémi Dufaitre, 74
Domaine Dugois, 100
Domaine Dupasquier, 126
Julien Duport, 74
Domaine Dupraz, 126
Domaine Dupré Goujon, 75
Domaine de Fa, 75
Domaine Le Fagolet, 76
Henry Fessy, 18, 76
Domaine Finot, 126
Domaine Jean Foillard, 13, 19, 46
Domaine des Fournelles, 76
Domaine Fumey-Chatelain, 113
Domaine Ganevat, 25, 27, 100
Domaine Genoux, 129
Domaine Giachino, 127
Château de Corcelles, 94
Château des Gimarets, 77
Domaine Mee Godard, 16, 18, 32, 47
Nicolas Gonin, 127
France Gonzalvez, 128
Domaine Grand, 113
Domaine de la Grand'Cour, 18, 48
Domaine Château de Grand Pré, 77
Château Grange Cochard, 18, 77
Domaine du Granit, 78
Domaine de la Grosse Pierre, 49
Michel Guignier, 78
Domaine Hamet-Spay, 78
Domaine Henri Maire, 101
Domaine Céline & Nicolas Hirsch, 79
Domaine Grégoire Hoppenot, 79
Domaine Hughes Béguet, 113
Domaine de l'Idylle, 128
Nicolas Jacob, 114

144

Château des Jacques, 3, 12, 17, 18, 19, 19, 49
Domaine Paul Janin et Fils, 18, 51
Château de Javernand, 79
Jean-Louis Dutraive, 48
Château de Juliénas, 80
Domaine Labet, 114
Domaine Labruyère, 80
Domaine Lafarge-Vial, 18, 81
Domaine Jean-Claude Lapalu, 18, 19, 52
Domaine Marcel Lapierre, 8, 13, 18, 19, 52
Château de Lavernette, 81
Domaine Léonis, 81
Thibault Liger-Belair, 18, 82
Frédéric Lornet, 114
Maison Jean Loron, 62
Château De Lucey, 128
Domaine Macle, 24, 102
Domaine de la Madone Le Perréon, 82
Domaine Louis Magnin, 32, 122
Domaine Manoir du Carra, 83
Domaine des Marnes Blanches, 115
Domaine des Marrans, 83
Domaine Laurent Martray, 83
Domaine Jean Masson et Fils, 129
Les Matheny, 115
Château de Mérande, 129
Yvon Métras, 18, 19, 53
Domaine Métrat et Fils, 18, 84
Domaine de Montbourgeau, 115
Domaine Famille Montessuit, 129
Domaine des Montillets, 84
Domaine Jean-Luc Mouillard, 116
Château du Moulin-à-Vent, 54
Maison Le Nid, 85
Domaine des Nugues, 18, 85
Maison Pierre Overnoy, 116
Christophe Pacalet, 85
Domaine Gilles Paris, 86
Domaine Partagé Gilles Berlioz, 130
Domaine Passot Collonge, 86
Franck Peillot, 130
Domaine du Pélican, 103
Jean-Yves Peron, 131
Domaine Laurent Perrachon et fils, 86
Robert Perroud, 87
Domaine Désiré Petit, 104
Les Pieds sur Terre, 116

Domaine des Pierres, 87
Château de Pierreux, 87
Roland Pignard, 88
Domaine Pignier, 117
Domaine Des Pins, 88
Domaine de la Pinte, 117
Domaine de la Pirolette, 88
Maison D. Piron, 55
Château de Poncié, 89
La Cave du Prieuré, 131
Domaine du Prieuré Saint Christophe, 32, 131
Domaine André et Michel Quénard, 132
Domaine Jean-François Quénard, 132
Pascal et Annick Quenard, 133
Château de Raousset, 89
Domaine Ratte, 104
Château des Ravatys, 90
Domaine Richard Rottiers, 90
Domaine Roches Bleues, 90
Domaine Rochette, 91
Domaine Coudert Clos de La Roilette, 18, 56
Domaine Rolet Père Et Fils, 105
Domaine Romanesca, 91
Domaine des Ronces, 117
Domaine François Rousset-Martin, 118
Domaine Ruet, 91
Domaine Saint-Cyr, 92
Domaine Saint-Germain, 133
Domaine des Souchons, 7, 13, 18, 56
Julien Sunier, 18, 57
Domaine des Terres Dorées, 9, 18, 58
Anthony Thévenet, 92
Charly Thévenet, 18, 19, 93
Jean-Paul Thévenet, 13, 18, 93
Domaine Thillardon, 18, 19, 93
Château Thivin, 18, 19, 94
Domaine de Thulon, 94
Domaine André et Mireille Tissot, 27, 106
Domaine De La Touraize, 118
Domaine de la Tournelle, 119
Château des Tours, 94
Les Fils de Charles Trosset, 133
Les Vignes de Paradis, 134
Des Vins d'Envie, 134
Domaine de la Voûte des Crozes, 95

Printed in Great Britain
by Amazon